Google Business Profile for SEO

2023 Boss Girls Edition
Your Ticket to Ranking on Google

#googlehacks
#digitalwisemedia

JENNIFER MARTIN

Boujee Publishing

Jennifer Martin / Boujee Publishing
8019 W. Grand Parkway, Ste 160-108
Richmond, TX 77406
boujeepublishing.com

Printed by Boujee Publishing
Printed in the United States of America

How to Use Google Business Profile for SEO- 2023 Boss Girls Edition
Jennifer Martin —1st ed. ISBN 978-1-7371733-9-7

Dedication

I dedicate this book to
My Favorite Italian Beauty Annalisa.
A friend for more than 23 years.
You have always pushed me to Hustle Harder, Love Myself,
and never let anyone stand in my way.

Thank you for being an unconditional friend to me.

You have stood by me no matter the problem,
through good and bad times, and always go above and
beyond to be the best friend to me.
Thank you for meeting me where I am and knowing what I need.

I love you, girl, and thank you for inspiring, encouraging, and
standing by me. Most of all, thank you for your friendship.

XO Jenn

Table of Contents

Introduction

In 2023 (GMB), now known as Google Business Profile, is an essential marketing tool that any brand or business can and should use. Through Business Profile, you can update your business information on Google; appear on Google Maps; allow customers to make reservations, get directions to or directly call your locations; and engage with existing and potential customers through their Google reviews.

But just how important is Google Business Profile?

Consider this customer reviews stat:

Approximately 76% of consumers check reviews
on Google before visiting a business.

How many times have you checked Google for reviews and noticed a business you were looking for had terrible reviews, so you continued your search to find other businesses with better reviews? Did you drive further to an establishment for dinner or service because another business had better reviews? We all have done it. It's the way we are wired these days.

Reviews are important enough to tell us how a business is doing, what we can expect from them, and if we want to visit them.

As you read reviews and see common problems others experienced, you mentally decide as your read if these issues and problems are ones you care enough about that would stop you from visiting this business, and you should find somewhere else. The ironic part of this process is that our mental evaluations are done subconsciously, and most of us do not even realize it.

Google is the largest search engine, and Google Business Profile (GBP) is FREE to all businesses. FREE.

So many things happen in our brains when we use Google to search for a business. The listing quality, our values, and the importance of what we are looking for all play a critical role in deciding where we ultimately bring our business. All of this happens subconsciously. So as a business owner, it is essential to ensure that all aspects of your Google business profile are complete using best practices and current trends. You want to consider all other marketing channels, but starting with your Google Business Profile is vital to ensure your business has a solid online foundation.

More than 65% of the people searching for businesses on Google are ready to become customers. This book teaches you best practices considering customer psychology to help ensure they do not subconsciously decide not to do business with you. I show you how to maximize your Google Business Profile, giving you Boss Girl Tips to ensure your listing becomes a solid foundation for you to build on the other marketing channels.

CHAPTER 1

What is Google Business Profile?

As a Boss Girl and business leader, ensuring your online presence is complete and top-notch is essential. What your online presence looks like represents your business to potential customers. Think about all the searches you do online. Now think about your opinion of those businesses when you see them online. People look at your website, your social media accounts, how many times you post, what you post, what is on your website, what your business listing looks like, how many reviews you have, what your description says, and so on. In just seconds, your potential customers have formed an opinion of you and decided if you are the type of business they want to do business with.

Use Google Business Profile to build a solid foundation for your online presence. So what is Google Business Profile? It is a free, multi-featured business listing that local businesses can and should use to manage their presence on Google Search and Google Maps. A Google Business Profile listing is not unlike online business directories such as Yelp (We Talk about Yelp in the book "The 7 Wonders of Marketing on the WWW"). Still, it is found directly on

Google and Google Maps search results. It, therefore, doesn't require a visit to a third-party site. Google Business Profile is considered part of Local SEO and Reputation Management and dramatically enhances your SEO.

Thanks to many features and functions, Google Business Profile has gone beyond a simple business listing and is a core part of local SEO.

Where Do Profile Listings Show Up?

Google Knowledge Panel

Information from your Google Profile Listing appears in Google's Knowledge Panel.

In SERPs, Google presents your information in a concise snippet form to give searchers a quick and easy means to get the information they need. It also provides your business with more visibility. Here's where you can find the Google Business Profile in the Knowledge Panel for a branded search:

Google Local Pack or Finder

The Local Pack is the block of business listings that appear below the map in search results. Shown after a user performs a Google search with local intent. Google constantly changes how many listings are shown, and sometimes paid listings are also shown in these results. Boss Girls and leaders who want to dominate Google should work to ensure they show up in these results.

Each business listed here shows up only because it has a Google Business Profile listing. Like the Knowledge Graph, all the information you can see here comes from the business's Google Business Profile listing.

Did You Know? You don't need a website to rank in the Local Pack — it's possible to show up here with only a Google Business Profile listing!

Google Maps

Google Maps is an app- and browser-based service on desktop or mobile used for getting directions and discovering businesses and locations.

Most consumers are familiar with Google Maps and likely have used it to locate a residence or local landmark at least once. However, it's also an important place for local businesses to gain visibility.

How do consumers use Google Business Profile?

Consumers use Google Business Profile for a whole host of reasons, such as:

- To find out a business's opening times
- To get directions to a local business or find its address
- To call a local business without needing to visit their website
- To write and read reviews about a local business
- To see photos of a local business and its products/services
- To visit the business website
- To make online bookings

- To view the available products and services
- To ask and answer questions about a local business

Who qualifies for a Google Business Profile listing?

Anyone with a business can qualify and get listed on Google. Boss Girls and Leaders- like Real Estate Agents or sole proprietorships can also get a Google Business Profile listing and absolutely should. In the terms and conditions, Google states that a staff member must be available to interact with your customers during the business hours you include to qualify for a Google business listing.

The Google Business Profile guidelines for representing your business on Google state that:

- Listings on Google Business Profile can only be created for businesses with a physical location that customers can visit or that travel to visit customers where they are.
- There is one case where a physical location *isn't* required. This is for service-area businesses (SABs) such as plumbers, pest control companies, cleaners, or any other service provider that visits and works at its customers' locations. Service-area businesses can specify the area in which they serve customers. For example, a plumber might offer services within a 5-mile radius.
- Online-only businesses and eCommerce ventures without a physical location that greets customers are not eligible for Google Business Profile listings as they do not meet Google's guidelines.

Google Business Profile Benefits Consumers

Google has worked to ensure that all its products are consumer-friendly. One of the ways they do this is to display websites and local listings that comply with their best practices and have updated information and search terms that match keywords in the listings and websites. There are other factors, but these are essential ones Google uses. The goal of Google is to ensure that all the websites displayed in the search results (SERP) have keywords that match the closest to the search terms entered and that the sites themselves are user-friendly. So there is no exception to ensuring your information is up-to-date and accurate. Google Business Profile listings help consumers in many ways.

1. Making it more accessible for searchers to source important information

    A business profile makes it far easier for consumers to locate information such as a business's phone number, address, or health and safety policies. With all this information easily locatable on a business's listing, searchers can get on with the important stuff, like working out if a business suits their needs.

2. Quick and easy local business comparison in one place is where subconscious decisions come in, and Boss Girls must ensure their listing is complete and updated regularly.

    Finding and switching between multiple businesses' websites can be a real headache for searchers. With Google Business

Profile, comparing businesses' offerings is easy by flicking between their listings.

This makes the searcher's journey far easier and means they can decide much more quickly. So, if you have high local rankings, offer relevant services, and give the searcher enough information, you could soon win a new customer.

3. Searchers can quickly check photos, reviews, and offers from nearby businesses. This is where you can ensure you have many images and coupons if you provide them.

Businesses can showcase their offerings, brand, and personality through photos and posts. With so much information available, these are the features that searchers pay attention to and make Boss Girl listings polished compared to others.

Knowing what a cocktail bar looks like (Does it have heaters in its outdoor seating area? How spacious is the bar area? Is there room to dance?) can help to inform searchers quickly. Reading relevant reviews helps the searcher understand if your business offers what they need.

4. It's easy to make bookings and appointments in Google My Business.

With the Googles Booking Appointment feature, Google Business Profile makes it easily accessible for consumers to get what they need from your listing. You can add apps to the listing to accept deposits for your appointments. In the case of beauty salons, spas, dentists, or other appointment-taking industries, this can be a handy function that saves both the searcher and the business time.

5. Google Maps users can follow and make lists of their favorite local businesses.

You thought Google+ was dead? Well, Google isn't done playing in the social and community space. Even Google Maps has a social function!

Users can follow businesses they like and create a list of their favorites. They are making it easier for searchers to keep up with their favorite local stores and support them.

When Maps user opts to follow a business, they are notified of Offers, Events, Posts, and changes to opening hours. Again, this saves time and makes the user journey much more effortless.

6. 'Justifications' make it easy for searchers to see how relevant a business is to their search.

Google Business Profile has simplified the search for relevant, nearby businesses. Thanks to the ever-evolving local algorithm, Google (generally) does a great job of surfacing the right businesses for users' search queries. As a result, finding the right business is easy.

If we search for a family-friendly restaurant, Google returns results where that phrase has been mentioned in reviews or even on the business's website (in the case of Bubby's, below). This function is called 'Justifications.'

7. It gives consumers ways to provide feedback and improve local businesses

Google Business Profile allows Google Maps users to provide their feedback on businesses through the app and validate the opinions of others, ensuring a more accurate picture of the company.

Through user-focused features like 'Suggest an Edit' or 'Provide Feedback,' Google ensures that any information on Google Business Profiles is as up-to-date as possible.

Crowdsourced features like Q&A, reviews, and even photos also help to provide a fair picture of businesses. All this contributes to simplifying searching for and pinpointing the relevant local business for a user's search. Again, these all come into play when subconsciously considering doing business with a local business.

Using Business Profile For Local Marketing?

So, we've established that Google Business Profile is not your Business Profile but rather a tool by which you enhance your Business Profile to boost its visibility and effectiveness. Let's cover the four core ways you can use this Google Business Profile to make your profile on Google Listing a better local marketing tool.

1. Engage with consumers

Consumers can interact with your Business Profile in many ways, and you use your Google Business Profile account to engage with them. You can respond to reviews, answer questions, enable direct messaging, and set up associated alerts. You can even use Google Business Profile to publish business posts, much like you would with Facebook and other social media platforms.

2. Highlight your business

A Business Profile alone contains limited information about your business. But through your Google Business Profile account dashboard, you can provide hours, a link to your website, products, pricing, attributes, and other details that make your business unique.

A complete Business Profile offers a comprehensive snapshot of your business, including its best features, right in the SERP.

3. Gain insights

Boss Girls use dashboard analytics to enhance their profile constantly. You can use the Google Business Profile dashboard to gain critical insights into your audience and local search performance. In the analytics tab of the platform, you can see the queries customers are using to find your Business Profile and whether they found you on Google Maps or Google Search. You can see a breakdown of actions taken on your listing and how your photos perform compared to other profiles in your category. Note also that there are ways to track clicks from a Business Profile via UTM parameters and Google Analytics. Look in the Boss Girls Tips at the end of the book to see how to use UTM codes and Google Analytics.

4. Perform local SEO

Just as Google has algorithms for ranking its ads and websites, it also has one for ranking Business Profiles. Through your Google Business Profile dashboard, you can incorporate keywords into your Business Profile and perform other optimizations to help it rank in local results, which are Boss Girl moves, and I will show you how.

Google Business Profile can help you optimize your Business Profile to appear in the coveted 3-Pack.

How To Use Google Business Profile For SEO?

Google Business Profiles are dynamic. Not only do they change form based on the platform, but Google prioritizes sections of your profile according to the searched term and the type of information most important to consumers in your category. Even better, Google encourages keywords in the content of your profile that it thinks are relevant.

Just as you (or your agency) would use a content management system like WordPress to optimize your website for search engines, Google Business Profile is used to optimize your profile and expand your reach. But it would be best if you prioritized keywords on your profile first. How do you use Google Business Profile for local SEO? Well, since optimizing for Google is essentially optimizing for searchers, it all comes down to targeting, quality of information, and trust.

Target your information

To use your Google Business Profile for SEO, incorporate relevant keywords into your Business Profile description to tell Google what you're trying to rank for. Use them in your "from the business" description, responses to reviews, answers to questions, and in the posts you publish. Make sure to incorporate them naturally, just like any other SEO strategy.

Include keywords in your description, editable through your Google Business Profile dashboard.

Maintain quality of information.

The completeness and accuracy of your Business Profile impact its rank, so make sure to provide the requested information in every section of your Google Business Profile dashboard. Essential here is your contact information, special hours, and attributes.

Build trust

The final approach to using Google Business Profile for SEO appeals to the trust component of Google's algorithm. Keep your information updated and accurate as your business evolves. Keep a steady stream of reviews coming in and respond to them. Also, signal to Google that you are active by regularly uploading photos and publishing posts to your Business Profile.

Reviews **and** responses appear on your Business Profile. Be sure to manage them through your Google Business Profile dashboard.

SEO is essential for any business, particularly for small businesses using local targeting to compete against large competitors on the SERP. Google is making local SEO even more accessible with its robust Business Profiles, so a Google Business Profile account is essential for any business trying to maximize visibility in its local market. Boss Girl Tip * It's Free!*

Get started with Google Business Profile today.

With a clear understanding of what Google Business Profile is, how it works, and how to use it, you can now see that using this free tool isn't just a good idea for local marketing but a must. Get your Google Business Profile account up and running now so your Business Profile can outshine your competitors and attract more customers on the world's most popular search engine.

CHAPTER 2

Setting up your Google Profile?

Set Up Your Google Profile

Adding your business locations to your Google Business Profile is more complicated than just entering your name, address, and phone number. (NAP) You'll often need to claim a pre-existing listing, verify your information, and choose the correct attributes.

Google Business Profile Login

Visit https://business.google.com to sign in or create a Google account for a business profile- use the same email login for all your Google products, and in the browser, you can easily access all of Google's products.

Once logged in, Google asks, "What's the name of your business?" (Below, we'll discuss claiming and verifying your business location in bulk.) You can search for a listing by typing the business name and address in the search box. Results appear in a list as well as on the map.

Claim Your Business on Google

To claim your business on Google, click "Add location" on the "Manage Locations" page. Google asks you for the name of your business. Type its name on the search bar and click on the correct name if it appears on the dropdown list.

If none of the results match your business, click the top of the list where it says, "Create a business with this name." You choose the business type: storefront (restaurants, hotels, etc.), service area (taxi service, delivery, etc.), or brand (products, brands, causes, etc.).

One note about service-area businesses: Google released a new update to Google Business Profile in January 2020 that makes it easier for them to sign up for a listing.

Google asks if your business has an office or store during sign-up. The "no" option allows you to choose your service areas before selecting your brand's category.

Businesses with storefront and service area locations can edit information for each site separately, making it easier for customers to find the right location.

Google Business Profile Categories

Categories are particular. If you're creating or adding your business to Google, you can choose from a list of categories to provide more accurate information about your business. For example, if you run Taco Bell's marketing, you can (perhaps optimistically) put your business in the "Mexican Restaurant" category. You can drill down into sub-genres like Tex-Mex or be as broad as possible by simply listing "Fast Food Restaurant."

If you manage a brand, Google recommends that all your categories are consistent across all your locations. So, every Taco Bell is categorized as a "Mexican Restaurant," and every McDonald's is a "Fast Food Restaurant." Once you've created your listings, you can always go back and edit your categories. Click into that location (or location group), then click "info" on the left menu. Once you see the details for that listing, click the pencil to edit, delete or add Google Business Profile categories.

For organizations with multiple locations, Google only allows you to have one primary category for each location. What qualifies for a multi-department listing?

However, there are some slight exceptions. For example, suppose you manage marketing for a chain of grocery stores. In that case, you can list your grocery stores and the pharmacy inside them as two separate listings, each with its primary categories.

Google's guidelines say you may qualify for multiple listings if your departments have separate entrances and customer care. Costco takes this approach to the extreme — listing its gas station, bakery, food court, tire center, and several other departments all separately. For businesses like this with one primary location but two distinct operations that are different enough to warrant multiple categories, you may be able to add them as separate locations. Think about banks inside grocery stores. Or restaurants inside gas stations.

If your business has two (or more) distinct operations running at one location, see if you can list both under separate categories, allowing you to show up in more relevant search results.

Verify Business on Google

The next step is using the Google Verify My Business feature. You must verify to Google that you own or represent the business listing. Typically, the verification code is mailed to you (yes, by snail mail) – this takes one to two weeks. Once you've entered the code into your account, you can manage your local business information on Google. You can verify a business in other ways — email, phone, and Google Search Console — but these are usually unavailable. If you *see a phone icon and an option to verify by phone, Google recommends that over a postcard because it is* much faster.

Option 1: Verify My Business By Mail.

The most common way to get a business verified is through the mail. Google sends you a postcard with a verification code attached to it.

Click on the "Verify Now" option in your account after clicking on a business listing.

At the postcard request screen, check and ensure the listed address is correct.

Wait patiently. The postcard takes about two weeks to arrive, and it's important not to change any information during this time. Doing so delays the verification process.

Once you have the code, enter the account, click on the business location you want to verify, and hit the "Verify location" button in the menu or the "Verify now" option.

Enter the five-digit code and hit submit to finish the process.

Option 2: Verify My Business By Email

Sign into the dashboard, and choose a specific location.

Click the "Verify" button and select email as a verification method.

You should see a message in your inbox that contains a code. You can enter that code in the dashboard.

Click the "Verify" button in the email message.

Option 3: Verify My Business By Phone

Verifying by phone can be available if you click on your phone number after hitting the "Verify" button.

You must listen to the automated voice system when a call comes through your phone. The system gives you a code to enter in the code field. You must tap the "Call me now" option on the app and enter the code from the automated voice system.

Option 4: Verify My Business Instantly

Those already using Google Search Console for a business may qualify for instant verification. Ensure that the email used for the business profile account is the same as the one used to verify the listing on Search Console.

Only some businesses on Search Console might be eligible for instant verification. In this case, getting a code via mail is the best option.

Bulk Locations on Google My Business

If you manage several business locations (10 or more), you don't have to add them separately. Instead, you can use the Business Profile Bulk Location Management tool.

Just visit the Google Business Profile Locations page to upload locations from a spreadsheet and edit the information associated with each site. (Note: You'll have to use this function from the classic mode because it's not yet available in the new version).

It would help if you made sure all locations meet the following quality standards:

- The business must make in-person contact with customers during its stated hours.
- The business must be open to the public.
- You may only enter locations under construction or not opened.
- You must be the owner of the business or an authorized marketing representative.
- Your listing name must match your real name, as represented by your offline marketing material, such as signage, etc.

- All locations must have the same name unless the business's real-world representation consistently varies from location to location.
- All locations must have the same category if they provide the same service.

While you can use your regular Gmail account to start this process, we highly recommend creating a new account using an email that reflects the domain of the businesses to be uploaded. Using the business domain reduces the time and steps required to complete the Google verification process.

Add Descriptions to Google Business

Your Google business description is a summary — up to 750 characters — that appears when a user searches for your local business or checks out your listing on Google via a desktop computer or mobile device.

It's usually displayed alongside or underneath your online reviews and ratings on Google and your business' review snippets. (Review snippets are algorithmically selected quotes from Google users and local guides that provide information on the keywords most mentioned by your reviewers.) Add your Google Business Profile descriptions and sign in to your account to get started.

On your Homepage, look for an option to "Add a description." Alternatively, you can click on your Info tab on the right and look for the section where you can add your business description.

Add your business description, then click Apply.

Here are some more guidelines set by Google for when you're writing out your business description:

- Don't spam it. Use it to pitch your business. Focus primarily on details about your business instead of more information about promotions, prices, or sales.
- It would be best to be upfront and honest about the information provided, focusing on relevant and valuable content for your customers to understand your business. Do not include URL links or HTML code or exceed 750 characters in the description field.
- Avoid misspellings, gimmicky character use, gibberish, etc.

Google Business Photos and Videos

Your Google Business Profile photos and videos are deciding factors for attracting customers. These images are the first impression of your business. They can attract customers or drive them away.

Add Photos and Videos to Google My Business

Once a business is verified, you can add photos through your desktop account. You'll go to the menu and select the Photos section. You can upload any photo or video if it meets the following size and format restrictions. Click on the blue "+" button to start adding your media:

Google Business Profile Photo Size and Format

Images can either be in a JPG or PNG file format and at least have the dimensions of 720 x 720 pixels.

The overall image file size should be between 10 KB and 5 MB. Images must also be focused and show a well-lit area. You cannot use image filters or perform "significant alterations" to the photo.

In addition to general photos of the business, you can designate two images as the cover and profile photos. Profile photos are a distinctive way for customers to recognize the business on Google, while a cover photo shows "your page's personality."

Add Video to Google My Business

You can add videos so long as they are less than the 100 MB file size limit. They must be no longer than 30 seconds and use a minimum resolution of 720p. You'll stay in your listen's "Photos" section to do so. Above your current photos, you'll see an option for "Video" You'll use the same process to add video as you did to add pictures. Click the blue "+" button and upload.

Remove or Delete Photos from Google Business

Owners and managers aren't the only ones who can add photos to their locations. Customers can do it as well. However, there might be some images that don't meet Google's Format Specific Criteria. In this case, you can flag them so that Google can review and possibly delete the photos.

Within your business profile account, go to the Photos section and select the offending images. To bring them to Google's attention, click on the flag icon on the top-right corner of the page.

You can also flag images via Google Maps. Once you find the business and the photo you want to flag, click on the three-dot menu icon on the top-left corner of your screen and click the "Report a Problem" button. You might also see a flag icon on the top-right corner of the screen, which you can use to report the image.

Adding Services and Menus on Google My Business

Using Google Business, restaurants and service-based businesses can submit additional information and links to help consumers learn more about their locations. The process differs slightly for restaurants and service businesses, so let's start with restaurant menus. There is a Menu editor available for companies in the restaurant industry. To access it, click "Info."

Restaurants can use the editor to add menu items (dishes), including title, description, and price, and create multiple menu sections, i.e., appetizers, entrees, and desserts. You'll see two places that mention a "menu." You can either add a menu URL (that links back to a menu listing) or add menu items to your listing.

This feature is only available if the listing is not currently connected to a third-party provider and for listings in English-speaking locales. If you run a service company, your experience is similar. Click the "Info" section of the listing for that location, scroll down, and see a place to add Services to your listing (and potentially an appointment URL if you have an online booking).

If you click to add Services to your listing, you are prompted to add a service item, description, and price:

Menu, Services & Links Appear Automatically

Google works with select third-party providers that provide booking and ordering services for local businesses. Links to specific booking and ordering services can appear automatically with your business listings in Google Search and Google Maps. These links are updated automatically via third-party providers. There's no way to add, edit, or remove these links in Google Business Profile.

Links for third-party providers display because of your business's established relationship with them. These links lead to the website of the third-party provider. From the third-party website, users can take action such as 'place an order or 'make an appointment or reservation.'

If you want to remove or fix a link in your listing, please get in touch with the third-party provider's support team or a technical contact to request the removal of your data from the information they are sending Google.

Managing Google Business Profile

- Add or Change Your Hours
- You can let customers know when your business location is open.

To add or change your business hours on Google:

- Sign into your account and click the Info tab from the Menu.
- Look for the "Add hours" options on your Info page or the section showing your current operating hours.
- Click on the Hours icon, which resembles a clock.
- Select the opening and closing hours for each day you are open. Click on the days that your location is available to customers. Finalize the hours by clicking Apply.
- Add Holiday Hours

You can also indicate holiday hours for each location. To do so:

- Sign in and open the location you'd like to manage if you have multiple locations.
- On the info tab, click the "Special Hours" section. You'll only see this section if you have already provided regular hours.
- Click "Confirm hours" next to an upcoming holiday or "Add new date" to choose a different date.
- Enter the opening and closing times for that day. Select "Closed" to indicate that the location is closed all day. If you're open 24 hours, click "Opens at" and select "24 hours" from the dropdown menu that appears. If you enter closing hours past midnight, set them correctly.

When you've finished entering all your special hours, click "Apply." Your special hours appear to customers on Google only for the designated days.

It's a good idea to confirm your hours for official holidays, even if those are the same as your regular hours. This way, you'll clarify that your holiday hours are accurate to customers. Remember that special hours can only be entered if you provide normal hours.

Google Business Profile Posts

Your Google business listing also acts as a content feed through which you can create and post up-to-minute content for your audience. The content can be text, video, or photo, which customers see when they find your business listing on Google. To create and publish Google Business Profile posts:

Sign in to your Business Profile. Open the location you'd like to manage if you have multiple locations. (Currently, posting is only available for individual business locations, meaning you cannot post content in bulk; you'll have to create and post location-level content for each location you manage on Google Business.)

- Click "Posts" from the menu.
- The "Create post" screen appears. Choose the post type you'd like to create from the following options: Update, Event, Offer, or Product.
- Add photos, videos, text, events, or offers to your post.
- Click Preview to see a preview of your post. If you're happy with your preview, click Publish in the top right corner of the screen. If you'd like to change your post, click Back on the top left of the screen to continue editing your draft until it's ready to publish.
- Add the Google Business Profile Bookings Feature

Google Business Profile also has a Bookings feature called Reserve with Google that allows businesses that use a supported scheduling partner to see insights and other information on the bookings received from Google. The Bookings feature is available in the U.S. for restaurants and businesses in the fitness or beauty vertical that use a supported scheduling partner. If it is known, go to the Home menu for a listing and look for the "Bookings" card:

Here is a list of Google's booking or scheduling partners:

To add this feature to your Google Business Profile account:

- Sign into Google Business Profile. Click on the specific location for brands with multiple locations to activate bookings.
- Click on the "Bookings" option within that location and sign up with the booking provider of your choice.
- Sign up with the provider of your choice.

- Within one week, your scheduling account is automatically linked to your Google Business Profile account.

After linking, you can receive bookings through Google. You're automatically eligible for bookings if you already use a scheduling provider. You'll see your booking history with that provider for bookings made in Reserve with Google in your Google Business Profile account on the bookings tab. Note: Your scheduling provider may apply fees for booking through Google. Check with your provider for more details.

Generate Leads Using Google Business Profile

There's a lot to say about lead generation and Google Business Profile. We recommend reading the in-depth guide about using Google's business to generate leads. But for starters, you'll want to make sure you get the most out of your account by taking these steps:

Connect Business Profile with Google Analytics

If you have multiple locations, ensure each location's "website" link sends users to the page for that specific location and not your brand's home page.

Add a UTM parameter to track the traffic coming to your website through your listing.

Optimize a listing for lead capture by including (if possible) integrations for:

- Making reservations
- Placing an order
- Scheduling an appointment

Make sure the website you link on your listings is optimized to convert GBP traffic by including multiple calls to action, including:

- Setting a reservations
- Contact you
- Visit the business

Track the leads through GBP Insights with specific metrics such as:

- Number of web visitors getting directions to your business
- Number of phone calls
- Turn On Messaging and Chat with Customers

Google Business Profile lets you chat directly with customers who find your business listing on Google Search. Responding to customers can help you answer their questions, tell your business's story, and attract more people to your location. **Please note** that messaging or chatting with customers is a new Google Business Profile feature available in select countries.

Turn On Messaging via SMS

To turn on messaging with customers:

- Sign into Google Business Profile and look for the "Messages" card in the Home menu.
- Click on the "Settings" button within the "Messages" tab to turn to message on or off. For new GBP users, click the "Turn on messaging" option.

Questions and Answers

With Google Business Profile Questions and Answers, you can ask or answer questions from any device and Google Maps on Android devices. As the listing manager, you have the most reliable answers to your customers' questions. So, it makes sense that you want to be the one to receive and respond to these questions every time someone sees your business information on Google. Unfortunately, listing managers don't get any notification when new questions about a location are asked. That means you'll have to stay vigilant and check your listings as they appear on Google or look inside your info for each location to see if there are any new Q&As. To check for any new Q&As and to answer any outstanding questions:

Under "Questions & answers," click See all questions in the info card for the place on the right.

- Next to the question, click Answer.
- To edit or delete your answer, click More and Edit or Delete.
- The person who asked will get a notification after you've answered.

- Fix Incorrect Business Information on Google
- Sometimes, you'll find that the information in your Google listing is outdated, inaccurate, or incomplete. It could be that your listing was created initially by a Google user but hadn't been verified. Or the business might have moved locations. Or you're taking over an existing listing to correct a few errors.

Ensuring that your business information on Google is accurate and up to date should be part of your online marketing and local search strategy. A simple search can help you quickly identify any inaccuracies or incorrect information about your business online. To fix your business information on Google:

- Add your business listing.
- Verify your business listing.
- Edit your business information.

Once you've added and verified a listing, editing your listing should be as simple as clicking the pencil icon in the "Info" section for each listing. If you've begun the verification process and need to fix incorrect business information while waiting for your verification postcard, you can also report a problem in Google Maps.

Do More with Google My Business

You must know additional Google features that work with your listing to get the most out of your account. These features can help your brand stand out from the local competition.

Google Local Guides

Google Local Guides is a global community of the top reviewers on Google. Think of it as Google's version of Yelp Elite. The more reviews a user writes and posts on Google, the more benefits they enjoy. If you get a review from a Google Local Guide, it's more likely to appear at the top of your reviews when a user clicks on your listing. That may be because Google gives particular preference to Google Local Guide reviews or simply because these reviews tend to be longer and include photos. Benefits of the Local Guides program include: special badges and levels, access to a monthly newsletter, invites to members-only contests, the ability to join Hangouts with worldwide tastemakers, connoisseurs, and Googlers, and eligibility to test new Google products and services before public release, invites to exclusive events, parties, and meetups, and annual thank-you gifts for high-quality contributions to Google Maps.

High-level Google Local Guides also get the chance to be featured on Google, Facebook, and Twitter. **If you're a business owner, you can still become a Local Guide** if you do not solicit Google reviews for a particular business and if you don't take advantage of the program for self-promotion.

What are Google Local, Google Places, and Google+?

These are the old names or brands Google used to refer to its services for businesses looking to manage their business information on Google. If you previously used Google Local, Google Places for Business, Google+ Local, or Google+ Pages Dashboard to manage your business information, your account has been automatically upgraded to Google Business Profile.

Add Your Business on Google Maps

If a business you own or manage isn't appearing in Google Maps, you can add and claim your business listing using Google Business. Once you've verified your business, you can edit business information like address, map location, contact information, category, and photos. You can also fix someone else's local business as a Google user. You can suggest an edit, report the error, or add a missing place in Google Maps. You can add a missing place if someone else's business is missing from Google Maps.

The Local 3 Pack

One of the most prominent and sought-after positions in Google's local search results is the Google Maps Pack. Also commonly known as the "local pack" or the "3 pack," Google Maps Pack is a set of three highlighted Google-Maps-based results (it used to be seven) featuring the most highly ranked businesses based on the factors that determine local ranking (reviews, local citations, etc.). Up to three businesses are featured in Google Maps Pack results, but sometimes, you'll see a sponsored result alongside or above the three organic ones.

As you can see, Google provides crucial information about each business organically featured in the Google Maps Pack: overall ratings, a short business summary, location address, business hours, price range, etc. — plus a featured photo on the right side. The "local pack" or "3 pack" is displayed above traditional text-only or links-based search results — making it one of the most valuable pieces of online real estate across any platform.

The Google Pack grabs as much as 44% of the clicks from page search engine results.

How to Get Your Locations in the Local 3-Pack?

The first step to making your business appear as part of the local pack is to claim your business listing on Google and manage your information using Google Business. But once you've done that, you wonder *what's next*. The next step is to optimize your reviews. Locations that don't have at least 4 stars won't show up in the Local 3 Pack. But it's not enough to have high aggregate ratings. You'll also want to:

- Have a steady influx of reviews (recency is a significant factor).
- Have positive sentiment in the text of the review itself.
- Have many total reviews (in addition to the trust factor, this allows your business to rank for longtail keywords based on what your reviews are talking about in the text).

If you're still struggling to appear in the Local 3 Pack, here's a quick checklist to help you determine if your listing is on point:

1. Use your business name, but don't stuff it with keywords or your city name.
2. Correct inaccuracies or errors in your data and eliminate duplicate listings.

3. Be as detailed as possible when entering your business information. Include your business name, category, map location and service area, phone number, website URL, hours of operation, etc.

4. Write original and compelling copy for your Google Business Profile description.

5. Avoid addressing variations. Meaning: if your location is at "72 Southwest Road," then stick to that way of spelling it instead of using, say, "72 SW Rd." or "72 Southwest St."

6. Use a local number instead of a toll-free number.

7. Manage and respond to all your Google reviews.

8. Upload high-quality photos to enhance the visual appeal of your listing. (These may appear in search results, too.)

Always ensure your information on GBP is correct, complete, and up to date. Remember, business listings that have been claimed and are regularly updated on Google Business and boast solid reviews and ratings are most likely to rank at the top of local search and be featured in the Google Maps Pack.

CHAPTER 3

New Features and Updates

Google Business Profile is quietly positioned as the best tool for local businesses to improve their online presence, reach potential customers, get discovered, and continue communicating with new customers. The most effective digital marketing tool utilizes customers' tremendous adoption of Google Maps when using local services or products.

Google Business Profile is like managing a social media profile explicitly aimed at local businesses to improve search rankings with local SEO and customer reviews.

Google Business Profile is not going to disappear in any way. That was one rumor where we saw that's not true. It's just changed its name. It's already changed its name. If you log on to google.com/businesstoday, you'll notice the name has changed.

Everything looks the same. It just says Google Business, Profile Manager. So, you'll see that Google changed the name to Google Business Profile, and when you go to the dashboard, you'll see it no longer says GBP and now says Google Business Profile.

Manage Your Profile directly on Google.

With the recent update, Google pushes Business Profile's most valuable features to a more visible location – the search results page.

This new update allows you to access your Google Search and Maps profile.

Here is how to do this:

- Suppose you log in with your Google account that manages your Google Business Profile profile. You can access the Google Business Profile account by typing your business name in the search results.
- The new panel summarizes all the features you can interact with regularly in the local search results. Now it is easier to have these options right at your fingertips.

Here is what you can do actually:

- View the latest reviews and star ratings
- Respond quickly to your Google reviews
- Create Google Ads – faster and much easier
- Create a Google post in a quick popup and promote your special offers
- View Google Analytics and insights
- Update your GBP listing, including business information, phone number, business description, business category, etc.

It's now even easier to view phone call metrics from the profile, number of searchers, search queries, new online reviews, etc.

Google Business Profile Messaging on the Desktop

As with other Google Business Profile features, the messaging functionality could be better promoted. It is available in the Google Business Profile app, but most account managers still need to learn about the app's existence.

But Google is making progress on that front and has provided the same mobile app chat option inside the desktop dashboard beginning this year.

Here is how Chat on Google Maps works:

When messaging is enabled, customers see a "Chat" button on their Google Maps Business Profile and can message you anytime.

This is an excellent addition to the tool suite as most small businesses spend lots of time in front of their computer and quickly answer questions from potential users with the chat open.

Here is a quick step-by-step on how to chat with customers on Google Maps using the new shortcuts in Google Search.

1. Search for your brand in Google search, so it provides the SERP shortcuts
2. Click on 'Customers.'
3. In the popup, choose **Messages**

Here on the chat screen, you can reply to the customers who requested information on your profile. To ensure an excellent experience for your customers, follow the chat guidelines.

Covid -19 Updates

Google has rolled out a new feature where businesses can ask for the financial support of their customers via gift card purchases or donations.

Utilizing the COVID-19 Support feature in the posts section of the GBP back end, owners can create a post that includes a gift card and donation links for customers accompanied by a short message from the business.

As of June 2020, Google supports the following providers: for gift card purchases, the business website, Square, Toast, Vagaro, and Clover; for donations, GoFundMe, and PayPal.

To be eligible for this feature, the business must have a physical storefront, and the listing must have been verified before March 1, 2020.

COVID-19 Scheduling, Hours, and Posts

With social distancing requirements changing how we do business, many businesses have adjusted their operations and hours. Google has revamped existing and new features to allow business owners to share these changes with their customers. In the back end of Google Business Profile, listing managers can update their online estimate links and business hours and add a COVID-19 post.

The Online Estimate feature draws attention to the Appointment Links section of the listing. Selecting the Online Estimate button auto-fills your existing URL if your business uses the Appointment

Link feature. If your company does not already still need it, you are prompted to one to the appropriate page on your website.

Business hours can be updated in three locations in the GBP back end, regular business hours, special hours (for holidays, etc.), and under the newest feature – More Hours. The More Hours section allows a business to describe business operations such as delivery, takeout, and drive-through. The primary dining services may be closed for restaurants, but using the More Hours section alerts customers of these socially distant services.

Adding a COVID-19-specific post to your Google Business Profile profile is another new feature Google has rolled out because of the pandemic. Below the business name and website link, these posts are prioritized at the top of your GBP. Under the Posts tab in the back end, users can select the "COVID-19 Update" option to highlight business updates related to the virus.

Attributes

Details provide customers with helpful information about your business, featuring amenities such as online scheduling and wifi or wheelchair accessibility if the company is women- or veteran-led. Under the Info section in GBP, owners can now list attributes of their business as another way to stand out to customers and highlight specific services, features, and other business qualities. The availability of these attributes depends on the type of business you operate, ensuring different companies provide relevant information to their industry.

Below is a list of some of the Attributes Google Business Profile currently offers. Remember that your business category determines your business profile's available attributes, so you only see some of these.

- Accessibility
  - Wheelchair-accessible elevator
  - Wheelchair-accessible entrance
  - Wheelchair-accessible parking lot
  - Wheelchair-accessible restroom
  - Mobility scooter rental

- Amenities
  - Gift wrapping
  - Online scheduling
  - Wifi (Free or Paid)
  - Restroom
  - Unisex restroom
  - Bar onsite
  - Good for kids
  - Restaurant
  - Baggage storage

- Highlights
  - Veteran-Led
  - Women-Led
  - Active military discounts
  - Live performances
  - Play area

- Offerings
  - Same-day delivery
  - Assembly service
  - Installation service
  - Repair services
  - Coat check
  - Help desk

- Payments
  - Cash only
  - Checks
  - Credit Cards (American Express, China Union Pay, Diners Club, Discover, JCB, MasterCard, VISA)
  - Debit Cards
  - NFC mobile payments

- Planning
  - LGBTQ friendly
  - Transgender safe space

Shortname

Sharing your GBP profile is now easier than ever. The short names feature has cleaned up long, messy URLs. Located in the Info tab on GBP, you can add a short name for your business by clicking on the @ symbol. Once completed, you can share your new, clean listing URL. As of April 2022, If you already have a short name, you can keep it- but you can no longer get a new one or change the one you have.

Service Areas

Need help with local SEO because your business doesn't have a physical location? The new Service Areas feature on GBP addresses that problem. Service Area Businesses can now define their service areas by region, city, or ZIP code without having a physical business address.

Products

Google recently rolled out its new Products feature, allowing businesses to catalog their products on their GBP profile. Users can scroll through a carousel of product images, each opening into their page with more details, pricing, and related products from your business. This feature is a great way to stimulate consumer interaction without leaving your profile.

Each product page is an opportunity for a link to its relative page on your business' website. Products can be grouped into Collections, allowing companies to organize the listing as they see fit.

Social Icons

Google Business Profile has been hot and cold about linking social profiles to local business listings, but they are here to stay! At the bottom of the knowledge panel, icons for Facebook, Instagram, LinkedIn, Twitter, YouTube, Myspace, Pinterest, SoundCloud, and Tumblr can be displayed. Adding these social links deviates from the norm, requiring some quick coding to alert Google to which social profiles are associated with your business website. With the help of

Google's Structured Data Markup Helper, generating this code is as easy as copying and pasting after your site's <header> code.

Google Marketing Kit

The Google Marketing Kit allows businesses to showcase outstanding customer reviews from Google Business Profile on other platforms and in real life! Users can create custom posters, social posts, and videos highlighting 5-star reviews and further business details. The Google Marketing Kit even offers free stickers to businesses that promote interaction with their GBP profile, inviting customers to review, follow or book with the company on Google.

Photos & Videos

GBP now offers businesses more control over photos displayed on their profile. Businesses can choose the logo and cover photo highlighted at the top of the GBP listing and various additional pictures throughout. Logos were previously only displayed at the top of the listing but featured on Google Maps and search results.

Appointment URLs & Online Reservations

Google Business Profile now features the ability to provide a second link to your site, known as the Appointment URL. This link is to direct search users to the place on your site where they can schedule an appointment, place an order, or contact you for more information. User experience is prioritized with this feature, as they are sent exactly where they want to go – minimizing the time users click around your site searching for your contact page or form. For businesses that offer Online Reservations, GBP partners with your site to allow users to book without ever leaving your listing!

- APP Exclusive Features
- Welcome Offers

Welcome Offers are a new feature available exclusively to business owners who utilize the Google Business Profile app. Owners can now create remarkable Welcome Offers to incentivize search users on any platform to become new business followers by offering a unique promotion.

Request a Quote Communications

Google has rolled out a new messaging feature that allows search users to contact businesses directly without leaving the Google Business Profile listing. Business owners can now communicate with their customers directly from their GBP app. Once this feature is turned on, a "Request a Quote" or "Get a Quote" button appears on the GBP. When clicked on, the button prompts users to select a Service Type, Date, and Time (When), input their Zip Code, and provide optional project details. Service Types are determined based on the business listing that has already been provided.

CHAPTER 4

Improve Your Profile Ranking?

Why optimize You Business Profile listing?

As a business, you're probably spending money on Google ads and website SEO optimization, so it's more searchable and gets enough traffic.

But you might – like many other businesses – overlook your Google Business Profile presence. This also means missing out on all the local SEO benefits it can bring you (and we'll look at those in a second, which is entirely FREE to use.

And if that's the case, you're not alone. One research study showed that business profiles on Google get just a tiny fraction of the overall billions of monthly views from Google searches. But not because Google Business Profile is just ineffective. Instead, businesses fail to take advantage of all it offers.

How to optimize your Profile listing?

First, claim it for your business (if you haven't yet)

If your business has been on the market for some time, the listing already exists (if you're unsure, try Googling yourself). And that's even if you haven't created it yourself. But you can't optimize it until you've officially claimed it.

If you don't have a Google Business Profile Account, you can create one at https://www.google.com/business after logging in with your Google account. Carefully complete all the sections of your Google Business profile.

Provide your potential customers with all the relevant info, including:

Your business name

Industry Category (for example, mine's "Marketing consultant"). This is important if you want to get found in relevant discovery searches when people search for a specific product or service in the area rather than your business name.

Hint: you can have more than one category.

Physical address

(if relevant, especially if you have a physical location people can visit, and not just an address for your online business – like me. Google asks you about that, too).

Business hours

Hint: Add weekday and holiday hours, so they're always relevant.

Your service area

(if you provide services outside your physical location).

Contact information

Including phone number and website address (and don't forget, your Google Business Profile account, though helpful, is not a replacement for your actual website.) So make sure you have a website also.

Appointment links

Products

Services

Attributes – to make your profile even more relevant. For example, I could go for "Identifies as women-owned" and add "Online appointments" to the service options.

Your business description (up to 750 characters)

Photos Make sure they're high quality and show you in a favorable light (quite literally). Images are proven to drive more customers: Google says people are 42% more likely to request driving directions to a business if its Business Profile has photos and 35% more likely to go to its website.

For example, photos of food (and drinks) and the interior are a good idea if you're a cafe or restaurant.

<u>Opening date (if relevant).</u>

Remember that Google verifies all the info and updates, claiming to take up to 3 business days for the verification.

Keep your Google Business Profile profile active.

You should regularly post new information – updates, special offers, discount codes, new service launches, etc. Think of it as another social media profile for your business – one people easily find in search results (as opposed to all the other social networks, which makes it all the more critical).

Things you can post:

- Special offers
- Product or service showcase
- COVID-19 updates
- Company news, etc.

You can add call-to-action buttons to your posts, letting customers perform instant actions like:

- Buy a product
- Book a service
- Order online
- Sign up
- Or call you, and more.

Keeping your profile active with engaging, relevant, and regular posts helps you engage your customers before they decide to buy or book from you.

Since they're already qualified leads when they reach your profile (most likely looking for you or a business like yours in the area and interested in what you must sell), it's your unique opportunity to capitalize on this with additional engagement.

Make sure your NAP is accurate.

Let's begin with the basics. For your Google Business Profile to do well with search engines and searchers, you'll need your NAP (name, address, and phone number) to be accurate. By accurate, we mean that it should reflect what your business is called. What word is printed on your signage, business cards, or website? That's what you should be using!

Write the perfect business description.

In your listing, you'll have the option to add a 750-character description. This is your opportunity to tell searchers about your business. The description is one of the first things you influence potential customers to see when they visit your Google Business Profile listing, so it's essential to get it right.

Try to include any USPs that your business offers. For example, if you run a pizza place in New York, do you provide plant-based toppings or gluten-free crusts?

Choose the Right Category & Subcategory

One of the most critical aspects of Google Profile SEO is picking the right primary category.

Did You Know? Local SEO experts say the primary GBP category is the number one local pack ranking factor.

Only your primary category is visible on your business listing, but subcategories inform whether your listing surfaced for local queries, so they're essential, too. Here's where your primary category appears in a GBP Knowledge Panel:

Picking a category might sound simple, but with so many choices, it can take time to choose the right one. We suggest checking out what categories your competitors use.

Upload amazing photos

To help searchers better know your business, Google encourages you to upload photos to your listing.

Uploading photos to your Google Business Profile will not only help your listing look more active and alive, but it's also likely to convert searchers.

To get the most out of this Google Business Profile feature and increase your chances of converting searchers, Google recommends businesses upload the following:

- At least three exterior solid photos, taken at different times of the day and showing the approach to the business from common angles

- A minimum of three interior photos
- Product photos for the most popular products and services you offer
- One image of any common areas your business may have, such as the reception
- A minimum of three management and team photos
- For bars, restaurants, and cafes, images of the most popular food and drinks
- For hotels, images of guest rooms should be uploaded
- As well as bulking out your listing with your photos, you can (and should) encourage customers to take and share pictures of your business.

Set Up a Booking System

Google's appointment-booking function is one of the contributing factors in the rise of zero-click searches. Now, searchers don't need to visit your website (or a third-party booking site) to get information and act.

Does your business offer appointments and bookings? For example, are you a hairdresser? A beauty salon? Or a service-area business? Great. You'll likely want to set up a 'Book an Appointment button to appear on your Google Business Profile profile.

If you're a business that takes appointments and bookings, this feature could make things easier for your customers and you. Make sure you keep up with any bookings that come through third-party systems.

Google Profile as a Customer Service Channel

If customer actions occur on your Google Profile, it makes sense to ensure customer service and support are available there, too.

It can be daunting to keep up with public-facing user-generated content aspects of GBP, such as reviews and Q&A.

Messaging can provide a way to manage the conversation behind closed doors and anticipate and provide damage control on any potential negative reviews.

Use UTM links & Call Tracking To Monitor Performance.

Once you're confident you're making the most of all the Google Business Profile features—and that your profile is optimized correctly—you'll need a way of tracking its performance.

Using UTM links (which stands for Urchin Tracking Module links) in the links you set in your profile, such as 'Website,' is a great way to monitor and attribute where visitors are finding your business and what actions they're taking.

If you want to track the performance of a page in Google Analytics, you'll need to ensure it is UTM tagged.

Above all, though, the best way to learn is to test and explore things yourself. Set yourself a reminder each week (or month if you're under-resourced and time-poor) to check out listings in your industry. What features are they using? Does anything look different? If so, test those features out for yourself and sees if it makes a difference to rankings or conversions.

CHAPTER 5

SEO & Keywords

A Google Business Profile listing is a must-have digital marketing strategy for growth if you have a business that relies on local customers. But this chapter is for you if you're new to search engine optimization (SEO) or not getting found as much as you'd like for local keywords.

Below, you'll discover the top tips for how to add keywords to your Google Business Profile. You'll also learn where to set keywords in Google Business Profile Profile pages to get the best results and how to change keywords not sending you the most qualified website traffic.

How to Add Keywords to Google My Business?

1. Add Keywords to Your Google Business Profile Description

The first step to adding keywords to your Google Business Profile is inside your business description. This is the easiest way to improve relevance for your Business Profile, a top-ranking factor in Google's algorithm for GBP listings.

2. Put Keywords In Your Google Business Profile Posts

The next step for how to set keywords in your Google Business Profile is to add them to the business posts on your Business Profile.

As explained by Google:

> *"You can connect with existing and potential customers through your Business Profile on Google Search and Maps through posts." And "Posts can include text, photos, or videos to promote Business Profiles."*

There are three main types of posts you can create:

1. Offers
2. What's New
3. Events

Add your keywords to the content each time you create a new post. That way, you can keep your Business Profile optimized for the phrases and terms that matter most for attracting the right customers for your business. This is also free to gain more organic traffic to your website without spending money on Google AdWords.

What's also good about these articles is that you can change keywords on Google Business posts whenever you see fit to improve your results. Also, remember that Google's content policy requires you to publish content that creates a positive customer experience. Therefore, you shouldn't post off-topic or irrelevant content to add keywords to your Google Business Profile page.

Business Profile posts should be relevant to your business and help your customers better understand your type of business.

Note: Posts over 6 months old get archived unless a date range is specified during the publishing process. So, make sure to keep your posts updated and fresh.

3. Get Customers to Put Keywords In Your Reviews

A powerful yet highly underused method for how to add keywords in Google Business Profile is to ask your customers to use them in their Google reviews (i.e., testimonials). This is a great way to increase keyword density naturally, too. You can also add keywords in your replies to GBP listing reviews.

Don't go overboard by including the exact keywords in every review response. Otherwise, you could overoptimize the review section and trigger a closer look at your Business Profile by the Google Business Profile Web Spam team.

4. Add Keywords In Your Business Q&A Section

Another tactic for adding keywords to your Business Profile listing is to use them in your business Q&A section. When a customer asks a question on your page, you can insert keywords into your answers.

5. Don't Add Keywords to Your Google Business Name

The final step you need to consider when optimizing your Google Business Profile listing for keywords is to NEVER set keywords in a GBP Business Name (i.e., business title).

Local search marketing experts caution against keyword stuffing in your business name because it can penalize or suspend your listing. Keyword stuffing refers to adding descriptors to your business name on Google Business Profile that are not part of the legal name for the business.

The digital marketing experts at SterlingSky reported that keyword stuffing the Business Profile Name could increase keyword rankings for a specific search phrase like "keyword" + [city] + [state], which is why this SEO tactic is attractive to Internet marketers.

However, SterlingSky also showed a few examples of what can happen to the rankings of a business when it was reported for breaking the guidelines by including extra keywords in the business name.

Google removed the keywords from the name of one Business Profile listing, and the rankings dropped from position #1 to #7. Another business lost the top #1 to #2 positions and lowered positions #14 to #15 for specific local keywords. But you won't always get so lucky with just getting a penalty. In some cases, your listing may be suspended entirely.

Google's My Business guidelines clearly state:

> *"Including unnecessary information in your business name is not permitted and could result in your listing being suspended."*

Therefore, your Google Business Name must remain consistent with real-world branding. Please don't risk stuffing keywords into the business name when it's not authentic to the legal entity name. Only include keywords in the business title when they're part of the business's real name.

How to Change Keywords On Google Business?

As with any search engine optimization strategy, you'll want to track, measure, and monitor your results with the keywords you use on your Google Business Profile page. And over time, you may determine that the keywords you're using are not attracting enough website traffic, the correct type of organic visitors, or qualified customers. In that case, you may be wondering how to change keywords. And the answer is simple.

All you must do is update the following areas of your Business Profile with the new keywords:

- Business description (swap out old keywords with new keywords)
- Profile Posts (use the new keywords in recent posts and consider deleting old posts)
- Q&A section answers (edit your answers to include new keywords and use them in new answers)
- As for the customer reviews, you'll need to educate your customers on the new keywords they should add to their testimonials for your business on Google.

Finding the Right Keywords for Your Google Business Profile Listing

If you need help picking the right keywords, the following tips can help. The most basic SEO method is to include the following type of keyword strings throughout your listing so you can show up for more organic searches and on Google Maps:

- [keyword] + [city]
- [keyword] + [city] + [state]

You can also optimize for the type of service or business you operate like this:

- [type of service] + [city]
- [type of service] + [city] + [state]
- [type of business] + [city]
- [type of business] + [city] + [state]

It's best to rotate through the various keyword strings and types related to your business so you're not using the exact phrases repeatedly. This SEO strategy helps you optimize for broader keywords to attract more customers.

You can also try to include "near me" keyword phrases in your Profile posts, as mentioned below. However, there's debate in the SEO industry on whether this method continues to work.

That's because Google can usually figure out your location by analyzing the local geographic coordinates of your computer's IP address or mobile phone with the GPS function. The algorithm can determine which business search results best match your location.

You can experiment with these keyword search queries and perform your testing:

- [type of service] near me
- [type of business] near me

SEO Must-Remember Tips

As you discovered, the best way to set keywords in Google Business Profile listings is to optimize the following locations on your profile: description, posts, customer reviews, and Q&A section. You can also change keywords to improve results. You may not get the best-ranking positions, the highest website traffic, or qualified visitors based on your current keyword optimization practices. So, refining your keywords, adding new phrases, and changing old terms is an excellent way to increase your business's visibility in the Google search engine.

CHAPTER 6

Google Posts

What is a Google Business Profile Post?

First launched in 2016, Google Business Profile posts allow you to share even more information from the search results page or your listing with your audience.

You can use Google Business Profile posts in many ways—to announce upcoming events, highlight new products and services, clarify changes in hours, share exciting news, or communicate your special offers.

Here are some answers to a couple of frequently asked questions about Google Business Profile posts:

Are Google Business Profile posts free?

Google Business Profile is a powerful, free advertising tool with the potential to funnel customers to your website and store from both Google Search and Google Maps. And posts on Google Business Profile are no exception–they're free!

Where do Google Business Profile posts appear?

Text, photo, or video posts appear to viewers in three core Google Business Profile locations:

1. The mobile view of your profile's "Updates" or "Overview" sections in Google Search and Maps.
2. Your profile's "From the Owner" section is in the Google Search and Maps desktop view.
3. Google Business Profile websites.

For example, adding photos to your business's profile will automatically show as posts in your customer's view.

Do Google Business Profile posts help SEO?

Yes and no. Google Business Profile posts don't directly help your SEO–but indirectly, they can. This is because Google posts can entice more users to click on your website by providing relevant and exciting information about your business, offers, and what you do. Increased clicks to your website and a higher click-through rate on your profile help your SEO.

Types of Google Business Profile posts?

The right type of Google Business Profile post for you will vary depending on your goal. Here are the five kinds of Google Business Profile posts the platform currently offers:

1. COVID-19 or Hours updates: This is a newly added type of post that Google Business Profile rolled out to accommodate ongoing business changes during the pandemic.

2. Offers: Think of this as the "promotional" post where you can display sales and offers from your business.

3. Products: You can highlight specific products in a particular "Product tab" where viewers can view your selected products' pictures, specifications, and other attributes.

4. What's new: This provides any general information about your business, like photos, videos, descriptions, or sharing new services.

5. Events: Share upcoming events your business is hosting or participating in with this post type. All events require titles, start and end dates, and timing information.

If your home services business is running a special promotion, the "offer" post would fit the context of the information best. On the other hand, if your vet clinic wants to increase brand awareness and share general information, the "What's New" post type can help you get the job done.

Because the content covered in each post will likely be different, it's a good idea to study and test the different post types to understand better how they'll look and which ones can help you reach your goals fastest.

So, you know how to create a Google Business Profile post, but do you know how to make one that gets results? Check out these top tips for your Google Business Profile posts.

1. Post Regularly

Google archives post types without an assigned date range over a week old. That's why it's a best practice to post on your Google

Business Profile regularly to keep your brand consistent and assure your customers that they're looking at up-to-date information.

It's easy to let this slip through the cracks, so your best bet is to schedule a short Google Business Profile session once a week or once a month where you can do a quick post and (plus, it doesn't hurt to make sure your GBP profile is looking good!).

2. Use High-Quality Pictures or Videos

Regardless of the type of information you want to share, leveraging videos or pictures is better; consumers retain 95% of a message in a media format. Creating high-quality photos and videos for each post is easier said than done, especially if you're a small to medium-sized business.

3. Keep The Text Short

One of the biggest mistakes Google posters make is using all the allotted characters, which is a staggering 1,500. Even though it's nice of Google to give so much space to work with, the ideal length for any given post falls between 150-300 characters.

Not only does this help hold the attention of viewers, but it also increases the likelihood that vital information is shown in the post without a user **having to click to read more.**

4. And include keywords in your posts

When writing your short post, include keywords that appeal to searchers to increase relevancy. If unsure what to write, put yourself in the consumer's shoes and consider what words and phrases would best grab their attention.

5. A/B test CTA buttons

Depending on your selected post type, you can add a clickable call-to-action button to your Google Business Profile post. Even though you cannot create custom CTA buttons (yet), Google gives you a fair number of options to work with. Try A/B testing CTA buttons to see which is most effective in getting people to complete your desired action.

6. Optimize Your Landing Page

Before you publish your post, optimizing your landing pages for visitors is always a good idea. Whether linking to a recent blog post, funneling users to a lead capture page, or even driving traffic to a new product, your landing page should be clean and aligned with your Google post. Lastly, ensure the action you want users to take is communicated and easy to find.

7. Keep it professional

Your Google Business Profile posts represent your business and maybe a searcher's first impression of you. Keep your posts informational, educational, and professional. Avoid "sales" or subjective wording to maintain professionalism within your posts and keep users engaged, so they act.

8. Proofread and Polish Up

Going along with professionalism, Google requires that your posts be honest and upfront, with no intention of trying to mislead or scam information out of users. Businesses' posts get taken down due to misspellings or poor-quality content. Taking the extra minute to triple-check that all the information you share is accurate, up to date, and revised accordingly goes a long way.

9. Get Familiar With Google's Posting Rules

Naturally, Google also strongly argues against content deemed offensive or violating another person or location's privacy. For example, posts with a phone number may be rejected to stop repetition since that's already on your listing. Avoid questionable content and stay within Google's guidelines by checking out Google's list of unapproved content.

Don't Wait! Start Posting on Google Business

Google posts only take a few simple steps and minimal time to create—most importantly, they're free! With this being such a local-friendly marketing tactic, it's a can't-miss for small businesses looking to serve a specific area.

CHAPTER 7

Insights & Analytics:

What is Google Business Profile Insights?

Google Insights is a free tool that shows how searchers found your listing and what actions they took on it. Information about your local search performance, such as the number of views your listing has received, how search users find you, and the types of interactions they have with your listing, such as clicking through to your website, calling you, or requesting directions.

Here's what Google Business Profile Insights looks like when you first land on the page:

Why are Google Business Profile Insights useful?

Google Insights is helpful for two core reasons:

1. It helps you understand how searchers find your business
2. It enables you to know what actions searchers take on your business

Beyond this, Insights can help you identify broader trends in how people find your business. For example, your cake delivery business might be surprisingly busy at the beginning of May, leading you to investigate providing unique Offer Posts for customers purchasing services around Mother's Day.

The more information you have available, the more you'll be able to improve your listing and encourage more actions.

How to use Google Business Profile Insights?

Now that we've established why Google Insights is valuable, we can learn how to use the data provided.

Here's how to find and use Google Insights:

1. Sign in to your Google Business Profile profile as usual.
2. The Home tab should load, and to the right of the screen, you'll see the 'Performance' box, which shows data from the last 28 days on Search and Maps.
3. Alternatively, you can click on Insights from the left-hand side menu.
4. The Insights data is split across several features, each of which helps you better understand your listing. Let's explore these.

How do customers search for your business?

Knowing how users search for your business isn't just a point of interest; it can also help you to make better marketing decisions.

You'll see three numbers at the top of the Performance box: Views, Searches, and Activity.

When you click on Searches, a panel drops down and shows you data related to Direct and Discovery searches.

What is a Direct Search?

A Direct Search is when someone heads to Google and types in your business name or address. You can draw a clear conclusion from this figure – these are people who already know about your business and have inputted their search with the specific intention of finding your listing or finding information related to your business, such as consumer reviews. Regardless of intention, these are people aware of you.

What is a Discovery Search?

A Discovery Search is when search users have typed in something generic such as 'plumber near me or 'convenience store open now,' and your business listing has appeared in the local search results.

What is a Branded Search?

A Branded Search is when a user searches for a brand related to your business. Google uses the example of someone searching for 'McDonald's' and being presented with a similar fast-food industry. The Branded Search category is only present in Google profile insights if your company has appeared at least once for this query.

Search users who found you through Discovery may or may not already be familiar with your business, but they haven't set out *to see you specifically*. These general searches typically relate to a specific need and the desire to find a product or service that fulfills that need.

So, what insights can we glean from these figures?

If the Discovery figure is smaller than your Direct figure, it's a sign that you must revisit your local SEO approach. A higher Discovery search number means you're visible to new customers rather than relying solely on people who are about you for web traffic and sales. Click on Insights in the left-hand menu to access this data in graph form.

Queries used to find your business

The information in this section, 'Queries used to find your business, can become a handy content optimization resource.

Available from the Insights menu, this lists the top search queries, which you can then use to confirm you're using the right keywords across your blogs, web pages, and Google Business Profile Posts.

Where do customers view your business on Google?

This section shows you where your impressions on Google have originated: in standard Google Search or from within Google Maps (desktop site or app).

What are Impressions in GBP Insights?

The Google Business Profile Impressions metric refers to how many people have viewed or seen your business listing. You can think of the number of Impressions as how many people your listing has reached.

You'll see two numbers here, Listing on Search and Listing on Maps, with options to view for the week, month, or quarter.

While this may not seem helpful at first glance, it shows you how well mobile optimization is going, mainly if you're working with a high-footfall business such as a restaurant or hotel.

Customer Actions

Next up is the Customer actions section. This data is excellent for helping you determine how to manage your listing and what to do next if you need more clarification.

This part of Google Business Profile Insights shows what type of action a search user commonly takes on your listing, including visiting your website, requesting directions, and making phone calls to your business.

You can use this insight to inform additional work on your GBP profile. A slew of direction requests shows an intent to visit your location. For example, this could lead you to create a Post sharing nearby parking facilities or bus stops. You can also edit the contact page on your website with directions, parking, and public transport access to help those planning a visit. You could upload additional images of your location showing the approach from different directions on the GBP listing itself.

Depending on the action, additional information may also be available. If search users have requested directions, for example, you'll see a map showing where those direction requests came from.

Directions Requests

When a GBP user has clicked on the 'Directions' link on your profile, you'll see a directions heatmap in GBP Insights, which outlines the location of those search users.

This heatmap is an excellent resource for local businesses, as it indicates where your potential customers are traveling from. This can help you better understand which neighborhoods to focus your marketing efforts.

Use the zip code and location data presented in the directions heatmap to hone your advertising and marketing targeting finely. You could, for example, use the zip codes to focus your Google Ads targeting or use this data to geo-target social media campaigns.

Phone Calls

If a search user has clicked on your Google Business Profile listing to call your business, you can monitor that data from this section of the Insights tab.

You can use this data to see which day of the week and time of the day generates the most calls from GBP – this information could again be used to fine-tune ad performance or help you decide when to schedule a new Post.

Photo views

As discussed earlier, photos are crucial to GBP performance and can affect how much traffic filters through your website from your Google Business Profile profile.

This part of the Insights tab helps you see how your images stack up against your competitors. You can see how often your photos are viewed and get a competitor benchmark, comparing your views to businesses like yours.

You can confidently continue to post similarly if your images receive more views. Fewer views mean you'll need to rethink your approach to ideas and do a little competitor research to see where you may be going wrong.

Photo Quantity

The photo quantity Insight lets you see how many images appear on your business listing compared to your competitors. If you have fewer images, take this as an indication that you need to upload more pictures.

Google Business Profile Post Insights

You'll check post views and likes when you write a blog post or update your social media.

Similarly, Google Business Profile Insights give you some data relating to your Posts in GBP –click on Posts in the navigation, and you'll be able to see how many new views your Posts have received in the week prior.

CHAPTER 8

Practitioner Listings

Google Search Results and Map Search Results help you find physical business locations, which are incredibly important for local search rankings. But what happens when your local practitioners get a lot of search volume...... can you optimize local search for individuals?

Practitioner Listings In Google My Business

Local businesses have been using Google Business listing to optimize for local searches for years. Still, individual practitioners have had a more challenging time promoting themselves. Now you can leverage Google Business Profile if you are a practitioner.

A practitioner or professional listing on Google Maps is for a person instead of a place. You may be eligible for a practitioner listing if you're a doctor, lawyer, dentist, realtor, or another practitioner who works at a local business.

An individual practitioner is a public-facing professional, typically with their customer base. Doctors, dentists, lawyers, financial planners, and insurance or real estate agents are individual practitioners. Listings for practitioners may include title or degree certification (e.g., Dr., MD, JD, Esq., CFA).

An Individual Practitioner Can Create Their Dedicated Listing If:

- They operate in a public-facing role (support staff should not create their listings)
- They are directly contactable at the verified location during the stated hours
- They (ideally) do not have multiple listings to cover all their specializations

Solo-Practitioner Listing

If you are a practitioner with one business location, working for one specific company (for example, a pediatrician that works at a single clinic), you are a solo practitioner. If your clinic has only one pediatrician, it is recommended that the business and practitioner share a single Google Business Profile listing and that you do not create a practitioner listing for yourself.

Multiple Practitioners Listing

If the business has multiple practitioners at one location, the best practice is that you have one Google Business Profile listing for the business. Then, if practitioners practice at more than one location, they can create individual practitioner listings. For example, if your pediatrics clinic has several pediatricians who all practice at other clinics, they are eligible to develop their Practitioner Listings.

Reviews For Practitioners

Google reviews are populated on a single listing. If someone leaves a review on the Places listing, it stays with that listing. If someone leaves a review on the Practitioner listing, it remains with the Practitioner listing regardless of the clinic/location the review is associated with.

An individual practitioner listing can provide an opportunity to show a Google Places listing for additional search terms, such as your name. Practitioner listings are not considered duplicates; Google will not remove or merge them. If a review is left on the practitioner listing, Google will not migrate it to the practice listing.

The listing title for the practitioner should include only the practitioner's name. It may also have their credentials identification or degree certification (e.g., Dr., MD, JD, Esq., CFA). The name of the organization should be excluded from this listing.

Ensure the practitioner lists links to a specific page, not the generic contacts. The landing page can have information about the individual or their specialty areas. In addition, the category should be more specific and different from the practices category to avoid competition with the practice listing. Practitioner listings should be distinct from solo practitioner listings or multiple listings.

How To Create A Practitioner Listing?

Log on to www.google.com/business and log in with any email address associated with a Google account, or you can associate your email address with a Google account as part of this process.

This is the start of the registration process for your practitioner listing. Register your name and credentials under "business name" and follow all the following prompts.

If you have not registered your office or name previously, Google shouldn't be able to find any search results. This is when Google will also verify if the listing has not been already listed. If it is, claim the listing as your own.

Complete all the required information, including name, country/region, address, principal business phone number, and category. Your category might be the type of medical practice you have, such as "pediatrician" or "cardiologist.

The final step is to get a verification code from Google via post, phone, SMS, or email (depending on your region). Google will not show your listing online until you've verified it. You can only verify it via the contact information you have put into your listing once you've done all that; congratulations! You are now all set to be listed on Google Business Profile.

CHAPTER 9

Google Knowledge Panel

Many brands want their own Google Knowledge Panel to stand out further from competing businesses, and it's because of Google reviews and its strong influence. Regarding customer reviews alone, Google holds 57.5% of all reviews, and 63.6% of consumers look at online reviews on Google before they visit a business.

With a Google Knowledge Panel, brands can give consumers more information and show off their services, convincing them to visit your business.

What is a Google Knowledge Panel?

Searching for prominent "entities" – think of major, well-known companies – on Google sometimes includes the Knowledge Panel on the right side of the screen next to the organic search results. Information on the panel can consist of a short description, images, important dates, social media channels, and the location of the brand's headquarters.

A great example of the Google Knowledge Panel in the wild is from Nike, which pops up on the right side of SERPs (search engine results pages) when you look up the company on Google.

Getting a Google Knowledge Panel can benefit any brand by establishing trust with consumers before they click on its website. Consumers want to make an informed decision before deciding on a specific product or service, and a Google Knowledge Panel can cement the purchase decision.

How to Get A Google Knowledge Panel?

According to Google, knowledge panels are "automatically generated," and information included in the panel comes from "various sources across the web." These panels are also updated automatically when new data emerges online.

Because knowledge panels are created automatically, there is no way for anyone to create their panel. With enough time and increased branding exposure, you can eventually gain your Google Knowledge Panel.

If your brand does appear, you can claim it as your own, but you'll need to be verified as an "authorized representative for the entity." To start the process and claim your knowledge panel:

Create a Google account if you don't have one to use.

1. Search for your business on Google and see if it has a Knowledge Panel in the SERP.

2. Scroll down to the bottom of the panel and click the button with "Claim this knowledge panel" written on it.

3. Review the information on the next page, which discusses the features provided to edit the knowledge panel if you are verified.

4. Sign in to one of the following sites as a final verification to authorize your representation of the entity in the knowledge panel. If Google can't associate one of the platforms below with the knowledge panel subject, you'll need to provide additional information to verify your account correctly.

   - YouTube
   - Google Search Console
   - Twitter
   - Facebook

Once verified, you can further authorize additional users to be your representative online and manage their permissions.

How to Edit Your Google Knowledge Panel?

Changing your Google Knowledge Panel can be challenging because Google uses an automated system to display updated and accurate information.

However, you can suggest changes to your Google Knowledge Panel if the current information doesn't accurately represent your brand. To do so:

- Sign in to the verified account associated with the Knowledge Panel.

- Turn on the Web and app activity settings on your account.
- Search for your Knowledge Panel on Google and click the "Suggest an edit" link (this is called "Suggest edits" on mobile devices).
- Click on the information that needs editing. You must submit suggestions for each item if multiple panel parts need updates.

A text box appears on the screen. When providing suggestions, include the following:

- Your suggested change.
- Why it should replace current content.
- Try to include any public URLs that confirm your suggested changes.
- Hit "Send" to finalize your changes.

If you don't see an option to suggest an edit on the panel, it's because of one of two things:

1. You are not using the same account to verify the Knowledge Panel.
2. Google doesn't recognize you as a "verified entity representative." You must verify your account or ask the primary representative to give you the same verification level.

During the review process, Google verifies your suggestions by corroborating them against "publicly available information on the web." If your changes are accepted, Google sends an email to you stating its intentions.

Differences GBP VS Google Knowledge Panel?

While getting your own Google Knowledge Panel isn't guaranteed, you can take steps in another direction to create your Google Profile, and it is displayed in the same place as a Knowledge Panel.

Just like the Knowledge Panel, you'll need to ask Google to "verify my business" before you can edit the information in the Business Profile, which includes:

- Business Name
- Category
- Hours
- Menu link (if applicable)
- Contact information
- Images

When adding these elements, ensure your information is correct and aligned with your other online listings. Listing inconsistent phone numbers, addresses, or even operating hours can hurt your search ranking on Google, which reduces your overall online exposure to potential customers.

CHAPTER 10

Google Reviews

Google reviews significantly influence how customers think about your company and are crucial for businesses looking to be discovered in search results.

By managing Google reviews, you can showcase your business in the best possible light and minimize the impact that negative reviews or low ratings might have on your brand reputation.

In this chapter, we'll discuss how you can monitor, respond to, and generate Google reviews and leverage these reviews to acquire and retain more customers.

Why are Google Reviews Important?

Google reviews are essential for one reason: your customers look for and trust these reviews.

According to online reviews statistics:

Google is the number one website for online reviews. 63.6% of consumers say they are likely to check reviews on Google (through

Google Maps and Search) before visiting a business location — more than any other review site.

It's easy to see why almost two-thirds of people turn to Google to find reviews of businesses. Apart from Google being the world's top website, zero-click searches are also on the rise. (It increased by 75% in 2023.)

(Zero-click searches happen when the top search results answer a user's query so that the user doesn't have to click through to a website or leave the search engine results page.)

The Link Between Google Reviews and Search Results

Google reviews directly impact where and how prominently companies and brands appear in search engine results.

A Moz report suggests that reviews are among the top factors influencing organic search results on Google and the top 3 influencing businesses featured in the Google Maps Pack. Regarding local SEO, more reviews mean more information for Google's algorithm.

How to Track Google Reviews?

The simplest way to find and track your company's reviews is to use Google Business Profile, the search engine company's free tool that allows business owners (or its representatives) to create and verify their data on Google.

Just click the Reviews tab on your Google Business Profile home page to see your Google reviews.

You'll see the page showing you all your reviews, which you can filter by "replied" or "haven't replied." You should still be able to see your reviews appearing in multiple places on the Web, such as Google search results and Google Maps, even if you're not logged in.

Receiving Google Review Alerts via Email

To help you track review activity, Google will notify you of any new reviews via email. The email notification includes review information such as the reviewer's name, star rating, a portion of the review text, and a link to the review on Google.

Why Have My Google Reviews Disappeared?

Ensuring that your Google reviews are displayed correctly on your business listings is vital to the success of your online reputation. You may be experiencing issues with a Google review not showing up for various reasons. This often has to do with one of two things: issues with your Google Business Profile listing or problems with the formatting of the Google review.

Google Business Profile listing issues: Inaccurate listing information, duplicate listings, inactive listings, and Google outages.

Google reviews formatting issues: Reviews marked as spam with links and URLs, fake reviews, and private or deleted reviews.

If the issue is with your Google Profile listing, you can make the necessary changes to remedy the situation. For example, if you have been inactive on Google Business Profile for a long time, all you must do is log into your account and start managing your listings again.

Responding to Your Reviews on Google

Online reviews on sites like Google give people a way to share their customer experiences not only with businesses but with fellow consumers, too. Consumers rely on these reviews to discover businesses and brands that provide the best customer experience.

Why Respond to Reviews?

How to respond to Google reviews is essential to managing customer feedback and protecting your brand reputation.

Customers care about your responses. According to online reviews statistics, 53% of customers expect a review response within 7 days. But as much as 63% say they have never heard back from a business after leaving a review.

Responding improves your online reputation. Customer reviews research shows that 45% of consumers say they're more likely to visit a business if it responds to negative reviews.

How to Respond to Reviews Using GBP

To respond to Google reviews:

- Log into your Google Business Profile account and select the location with the reviews you want to manage. Then click the Reviews tab on the listing's home page.
- When you land on the Reviews page, you'll see each review posted on your business listing organized (by default) by date. You can respond to each review by clicking the "Reply" button.

Please note that your reply is displayed publicly on Google and must comply with Google's review policy.

You can also edit your review responses to clean up typos or update what was initially written. Each review that has been responded to appears with an "Edit" button for updating your replies.

Remember that your customers get notified by email when you respond to their reviews. Your response is published immediately, and the email notification is sent to the customer approximately 5 minutes later. The 5-minute delay allows you to edit or correct your response after submission.

Why Is It Important to Get New Reviews?

A steady stream of new reviews can dramatically improve your search engine performance, which is essential to driving traffic and attracting more customers.

This makes it crucial for companies to learn how to get Google reviews proactively. It's insufficient to plant your business flag on Google and wait for your thoughts.

According to research, companies that proactively request reviews enjoy higher ratings (4.34 stars) than those that wait for unprompted reviews (3.89 stars).

Suppose you don't proactively request customers for reviews. In that case, your review data sample is more likely to be biased towards those motivated to leave a review: people with a customer service issue.

How to Get More Google Reviews?

Here are practical ways to get your company's Google reviews and build your brand's online presence.

Use Email

Do you collect customers' email addresses at the point of sale or care? If so, you'll quickly realize that email is one of the most effective ways to get reviews on your Google Business Profile. If you're managing over 100 business locations, using automation (instead of manually reaching out to customers) should help you save time and money.

One option is integrating your review requests into your customer relationship management (CRM) or point of sale (POS) system. If you send a message to customers, add a link to your Google business listing so that it only takes a few clicks to share their experience.

Another option is to utilize review generation tools within your local SEO software.

Send SMS Campaigns

You can also send SMS requests if you're syncing your point-of-sale system to send email alerts to customers. SMS open rates are significantly higher than email and can drive better engagement and more reviews.

Create a Google Reviews Link

Creating a unique Google reviews link and sharing it with your customers encourages them to review your business on Google.

Make Your Customers Happy

The easiest, most effective, and fundamental way to get reviews with 5-star ratings is to consistently deliver excellent service and create "wow" moments with customers.

If, on the other hand, you have customers who are not satisfied or happy with their experience, then make a point to reach out to them and identify and address issues.

What is Review Gating?

Unlike other business review sites (for example, Yelp), Google encourages business owners to contact their customers and ask for reviews. However, Google doesn't want businesses to discourage or prohibit negative reviews or selectively solicit positive customer reviews.

A practice commonly referred to as "review gating," this is usually done by sending customers a survey or feedback form — through email, SMS, landing pages, or social media. Based on their form responses, customers are then asked to either post a positive review on Google if they had a positive experience — or share details of their feedback privately if they had a negative experience.

Review gating lets brands filter out detractors from their online review generation efforts. This, however, is against Google's review policy. To meet the demand for transparency and authenticity in reviews, your company must clarify that customers can leave you a negative review.

Can I Share Google Reviews on My Website?

Yes, and we highly recommend it.

Showcasing your best and highest-rated reviews on your website is a great way to provide social proof, boost consumer confidence, and encourage user interaction. Reviews also often serve as the final push people need to convert from visitors to customers.

Put: authentic, positive reviews on your website and leverages the power of testimonial-based marketing. Letting happy customers make statements about the benefits of your products or services makes it easier for potential customers to trust your company.

You can display Google reviews on your homepage and show your company's overall rating. You can also create location pages displaying each business location's reviews. Another option is to create a customer testimonials page, which is a great way to turn website visitors into customers and loyal fans.

Can I Delete or Edit Google Reviews?

Here's the short answer: companies can't delete any reviews on their Google business listings.

Most of the time, Google Business Profile users who succeed in having a review deleted can do so because the review violated the Google review policy.

There is also no straightforward way to edit reviews on Google. Customers can change or update their reviews to reflect their most recent experience with a business.

Brands cannot edit Google reviews. If you disagree with your review, the best practice is to respond to the review or engage with the customer directly. This can even result in the customer updating their review in certain situations. Under no circumstances should you engage in a back-and-forth with the review poster. Look at our Reputation Management Chapter in "The 7 Wonders of Marketing on the WWW" for more information on managing your online reputation effectively.

Can I Disable Reviews on Google My Business?

Unlike Facebook reviews, Google reviews cannot be disabled or turned off. Every business listing on Google displays reviews.

If you're seeing low ratings and negative reviews appear on your listings, we recommend responding to the review and solving the customer's issue. To minimize the impact of the low rating on your overall score, you can reach out to customers and generate new reviews.

Should I Buy Reviews?

When building your company's online reputation, it can be tempting to take shortcuts and try to buy Google reviews.

Fake reviews violate Google's guidelines and will almost certainly be removed from your listing sooner or later. Regulatory agencies like the FTC also impose hefty fines on companies found to be buying fake reviews.

Google reviews are essential in how today's consumers discover and judge businesses. They can also shape a brand's online reputation and reveal valuable insights into its operations, showing areas where an organization can improve customer service and experience.

By tracking, responding to, and generating reviews on Google — and applying best practices in reputation management — you can improve your brand's search visibility, outperform competitors, and acquire more customers.

Google Business Profile is a great free tool for driving traffic and conversions with relatively low effort, and we highly recommend it as part of your larger digital marketing strategy.

If your business has a solid digital footprint, you want to ensure that you make the most out of your Google Business Profile listing. Good Luck!

Please send us a review on our Google Business Profile Page and comment about this book, what helped you, and your favorite new hack for GBP.

CHAPTER 11

Google Screened

What is Google Screened?

Another program by Google to verify local service providers is called Google Screened. Through Google Partner programs, Google's LSAs, as well as third regulatory parties and regional states, Google conducts thorough background checks. The verification aims to confirm that a service provider's permits, reputation, and insurance are current.

Before awarding candidates the Google green checkmark badge, also known as the "Badge of Trust," from Google Screened, the program's objective is to pre-screen applicants. This symbol indicates that a local company has met Google's screening standards and is now regarded as a Google-trusted provider.

It takes hours to go through thousands of search engine results when looking for financial advisors, real estate brokers, or attorneys online. Because more and more individuals search online for professional service providers, these businesses must try to stand out. While many businesses that offer professional services have relied primarily on positive online reviews to win customers, this strategy is no longer a sustainable source of website traffic.

Instead, service providers must think of creative ways to attract new customers because so many uses paid advertising and search engine optimization.

Creating an All-inclusive Marketing Strategy

It's crucial to diversify your marketing strategies. Professional service providers should develop their marketing strategy using a thorough methodology. Google Screened can assist professional service providers in growing their website traffic, but this will only do a little with a website.

Typically, customers decide whether to do business with a company within three seconds of seeing its website. Service providers should be given more time to create a favorable first impression. Even if they come via a Google Screened LSA ad, visitors aren't going to stay on an outdated, poorly-designed website.

** Boss Girls Tip- Make sure your website is Updated, Mobile Friendly, and optimized **

Professional service providers must stay on top of digital communications with new and existing clients and have a well-designed website. Communications may combine email marketing, social media marketing, sponsored advertisements, or other kinds of digital marketing, depending on the sort of business.

Getting Google Screened Certified

Google Guaranteed informs customers that a company satisfies Google's exacting criteria. Business owners must pass business-level and personal background checks to be eligible for Google Screened.

Google may additionally ask employees to undergo background checks depending on the sort of business. Google confirms that the supplier not only passes all the background checks but also has all the required licenses and insurance for their line of business. The service provider must also keep a Google rating of at least three stars.

Professional service providers can publish Local Service Ads after receiving approval (LSAs). The Google Screened notice and green checkmark emblem are displayed next to these adverts at the top of the search engine results page. Google Screened Advertising has a professional headshot in contrast to Google Guaranteed ads. This grabs attention and gives the company a more polished appearance. It also provides the advertisement with a personal touch.

Background Check for Businesses

Each business that applies must pass a background check.

Business-Owner Background Check

Each applicant must complete a background check on themselves.

Background checks on employees

In some cases, every employee (including independent contractors, temporary employees, etc.) who may render services on the company's behalf must also undergo a background check.

Checks for Insurance

Any category that calls for general liability insurance must additionally provide an active certificate of insurance.

License Verification

Business owners may be asked to present necessary state or local license documentation in certain situations.

This program is free for the business except for local service ad expenses, which vary from region to region. Local partners conduct all completely confidential checks. Your company won't be allowed to join the Google Screened program if it fails a background check.

Google Screened Application Procedure

Getting "Google Guaranteed" and "Google Screened" are similar processes. For starters, whichever option you select, your company name has a green checkmark on the Local Service listings. The application process is identical in that several screening levels are conducted.

Knowing that the Google Guaranteed Program is not free is also critical. The base membership costs $50 monthly (or $600 annually). This does not, however, account for the expenses related to each lead produced as a result of your advertisements. Depending on external conditions, costs may change, but the typical cost per lead is about $25.

Starting is relatively easy. Signing up for the program makes no sense if you want to use Google ads to expand your audience. Here's a step-wise procedure;

Step 1: Sign up for Google Local Services Ads

Opening a Google Local Services Ads account is the only way to get Google Screened. It only requires a few minutes, is easy, and is free. If you need assistance, contact the Google Ads customer care team; they are helpful.

Step 2: Get three stars on Google Reviews as the next step.

Your business must have a 3-star rating on Google or above to be Google Screened. However, you may legally ask for reviews from your customers even if you don't have any or your rating is below 3.

The brand-new SEC advertising rule that took effect in 2021 is helpful because it lets you invite your clients to use reviews (which you can use on your website and other promotional materials). The only issue is that you must establish that you issued the same review request to all your clients by documenting your request for reviews. Here, you can't pick and choose your best clientele.

It is simple and free. You must first register for Google Business Profile to receive reviews on Google and share your review link with customers. Then, take a few minutes out of your day to complete it if you haven't already.

When you submit your company's address, Google will issue you a postcard with a confirmation number to ensure you provided the correct address. Usually, that takes a week or two. The confirmation postcard is the only step of the GBP registration process that requires a little more time.

Step 3: Pass a few background and license checks in the third step.

Financial advisers must fulfill the following criteria to get Google Screened:

- Background check specifications
- Commercial check
- Owner verification
- A verified check
- Insurance necessities: General liability protection
- License prerequisites: Examination of each financial planner in the firm's licenses

Although the process is simple, fulfilling these prerequisites can take at least a few weeks. If Google rejects your company and you feel there was an error, you have 30 days to file an appeal.

You can begin promoting your company as being Google Screened once the checks are completed successfully, running local services ads and placing better in local searches!

You'll need to do a few things if you decide that moving forward with the application process is in your organization's best interests. First, gather all of your required paperwork and review it beforehand.

Check your reviews next to make sure they are portraying your company favorably. Address any unfavorable comments immediately if there are any. Then, join for Local Services Ads, complete the documentation, and submit!

Benefits of Google Screened Certification

Google Screened certification can assist service providers in keeping their current customers and helping them grow their clientele and outpacing their rivals. Customers who might otherwise shop around are more inclined to stick with the same company if they can tell they put in the time and effort to become certified.

It's vital to note that professional service companies can only run Local Service Ads (LSAs) with Google if they receive Google Screened accreditation. As a result, LSAs appear first in the search results, ahead of other paid adverts.

One of the critical elements affecting LSA's success is reviews. To guarantee quality performance, professional service providers must have as many positive evaluations and high star ratings as their rivals. Many companies find it helpful to request evaluations from current clients.

Although obtaining Google Screened certification requires time, the effort is well worth it. Professional service providers screened by Google typically appear at the top of the search results.

Credibility

The green checkmark shows that you have undergone a thorough investigation. Your local service company has been approved after a rigorous review process in which Google verified your company's credentials and reputation. That says a lot about the reliability of your company.

<u>Potential clients quickly connect the green checkmark with reliability.</u>

All Google Screened advertising includes pictures of the company owner, customer reviews, years the company has been operating, phone numbers, and other contact information. So naturally, customers gravitate toward images of the company founders right away, which is a terrific approach to establishing a relationship.

Increased Visibility and More Direct Leads

Ultimately, being found and enhancing a service company's visibility are the most critical factors. As a result, the searchability of nearby service providers undergoing Google screening will immediately improve. More crucially, Google's click-to-call function ensures a high volume of incoming calls, translating to more direct leads to close.

Finding an individual to perform a service is much labor. Consider how people approach finding the significant services they require. First, they'll conduct a Google search and read client reviews to determine which is reliable. They next get in touch with several providers and request references from each. These references are then called. Some people also frequently visit their local BBB to see how these companies are doing.

How Does Google Screen Help Firms?

The Google Screened initiative aids companies in developing dependable connections with potential clients. Businesses that display the Google Screened emblem attest that Google has approved them after completing the necessary background checks—giving customers more assurance that the company can achieve their expectations.

Because Local Service Advertising is given the most prominent position on the Google search engine result page, above all other paid ads, maps, and other components, they allow companies to successfully present themselves to potential customers. Additionally, Google Screened Local Service Ads improve your listing's engagement with various eye-catching visuals. These include the vendor's headshot, the company star rating, the number of Google reviews, your contact details, and—most importantly—the Google Screened badge, which draws in potential customers and increases click-through rates for listings.

When they click on the listing, a page with the company's details that are most crucial to customers when making a decision appears rather than the extra visit to the business's website. In addition, businesses appear in voice-command searches and hear confirmation that the business is Google Screened, thanks to Location Service Ads, available on Google Assistant, smartphones, and Google Home devices.

In contrast to paid advertisements, which are charged each time a user clicks on the link, Google Screened only charges businesses for qualified leads relevant to their services. This makes it an affordable way to promote businesses. Only phone calls that continue longer than 30 seconds are charged to prevent businesses from being charged for unwanted or spam calls.

Because Google has confirmed the service provider, the Google Screened Badge enables prospective clients to confidently book professional services like those of a financial advisor or attorney. Industry, not the degree of verification, determines the type of badge.

Develop trust

Professional service providers can easily keep track of customer feedback by following up with consumers and asking them to review and share their experiences.

How to Use Google Screened

Businesses that want to be considered for Google Screening must pass Google's qualifying and screening process, which may include license and background checks depending on the type of business. If your company is eligible, Google will display a Google Screened icon next to your company's listing, informing customers that Google has carefully examined and approved your establishment.

You can run Google Local Services advertisements once Google Screened has confirmed your company. Google Local Services advertising appears VERY HIGH UP in relevant Google search results, even before sponsored advertisements. Professional service businesses who use Google Local Services advertisements only pay for qualifying leads that result in actual business.

The Process of Local Service Providers Selection by Google

Although becoming Google Screened is relatively straightforward, the vetting and certification process takes a long period for Google to complete. Usually, it takes two to three days to complete each phase, with background checks lasting longer.

In addition, all submissions must be submitted through a digital marketing agency, a Google Partner.

Identification by taking a social security number and a legitimate driver's license form will be required from participants. Additionally, local service providers' copies of federal, state, and insurance documentation are necessary.

Employees may also need to be screened, depending on the exact size of the firm. Then, Google verifies all insurance needs by doing a background check on the company and its owners.

The most crucial step is to have a profile with Google My Business, having a total customer review rating of about three stars or above. Maintaining a good rating requires proactive customer feedback management because new clients will automatically choose the service with the best overall rating.

Lawyers Also Gain from Google Screened

We sought the best Google Screened program guidance from business executives and lawyers to assist lawyers in establishing a reliable internet presence. Several pieces of advice, such as getting at least one Review and upgrading your headshot, will assist you in building your business's internet visibility and bringing in clients.

The following seven Google screened hints for attorneys:

- A minimum of One Review
- The Badge Will Show the Public You've Been Verified and Will Increase Your Credibility
- Follow Up to Ensure the Screening Was Complete Nurture Customer Reviews
- Freshen up your headshot
- Give Specific Information

A minimum of One Review

Your Local Service Ads (LSA) must have at least one Review with an average rating of 3.0 to be accepted by Google (out of 5.0). You can incorporate reviews from your Google My Business listing if you'd like. However, conducting LSAs does not require that you have a Google My Business listing.

Reviews of your LSA profile are available right away. LSAs for law firms with more client testimonials and ratings will probably display more frequently. Try to obtain new reviews for your LSA profile and Google My Business listing.

Display to The Public That You've Been Assessed

Allowing Google Screened to conduct its investigation by verifying it will show the public that you are reliable. Combining the Google Screening program badge with the minimum three-star rating required by Google will help you attract more customers. People want guidance when making decisions, so letting Google check you out and publishing the results will help your business attract new clients.

Your Credibility Will Rise With the Badge

Google can screen lawyers as trustworthy business entities through the Google Screened Program. Many companies have used Google's Local Services Ads to advertise their products and services. Google now explicitly provides this option to lawyers and law firms in specific regions and practice areas. Law companies will generate more leads because clients will view attorneys who have obtained the Google Screened badge as credible. Legal professionals will stand out from the crowd thanks to the Google Screened badge.

Follow Up to Confirm the Screening Was Successful

Develop the practice of fostering positive customer evaluations to protect against negative feedback from angry customers. While directly requesting Google reviews may be in poor taste, you can encourage your clients to leave positive reviews. This action is possible by providing links to your page in later emails, posting a QR code in your lobby, installing a widget on your website, and sharing positive reviews on social media.

Freshen up your headshot.

In contrast, Google Screened will display your headshot before other search results. Consider it a dating profile picture. Both professionalism and a human connection are required. They must be motivated to collaborate with you. Be welcoming and smile! Using an outdated image or your most professional severe face is inappropriate now.

Give Specific Information

The Google Screened program can work wonders for your company's SEO, but to make the most of it, you must be specific and thorough with your information. For instance, specifying the number of attorneys at your company might boost exposure, and Google will construct profiles for them after verifying their license information.

Does Google Screened Make Sense for Advisors?

Google Screened is a strategy for Google to encourage more companies to run Local Services Ads, as you may have already surmised. That might be the case, and you might want to run those adverts, but becoming Screened is free, and you are under no pressure to do so if you don't want to. Although getting Google Screened may take a few weeks, the time commitment on your end is minimal, and no financial outlay is required—unless you choose to run advertisements.

The downside risk of this technique would place it somewhere south of twenty if we had to assign a Risk Number to it. Therefore, professionals using Google Screened to attract new clients should take particular actions to ensure their business or practice is ready. These consist of the following:

Making the most of their Google Business Profile page

Ensure that your page has been claimed, presents accurate data, and possesses as many features as possible.

Share High-Quality Content

Consistently share pertinent content on your Google page. If the Events or Offers function applies to your company, access and use it. These actions are crucial to the algorithm Google will utilize when rotating your listing in front of your subsequent potential client and will make your Google page stand out.

Ask for feedback

The main factor in being eligible for these Google Guaranteed Programs is reviews. So make sure you've put in place a method for gathering customer feedback and answering all of it, whether positive or bad.

CHAPTER 12

Google Guarantee

The Google Guarantee

Google introduced "Google Guaranteed" in Canada towards the end of 2018. The well-known Google Guaranteed program was launched to cater to neighborhood businesses providing residential services. The application is a component of Google's AdWords service. Even the Search Ads from Ads on Google can't compare to these listings.

This program helped small businesses and stopped bogus services. Businesses that complete Google's screening and qualification process receive the Google Guaranteed badge. Customers feel more secure and confident when making service reservations because of the unmistakable green and white check mark.

This program targets several home service segments via the Local Service advertisements feature. Customers receive satisfactory service thanks to this program, which guards against fraudulent services.

In this chapter, you can read more about the process, conditions and terms, regulations, and other crucial information about the reputable Google Guaranteed Concept Program. This program's initiative is vital since several local businesses stand to benefit significantly from it in the foreseeable future.

Only a few locations in Canada and the US currently have access to the service, which is still under active beta testing. Several screening procedures must be completed before being listed, and background checks and licensing or insurance verification, as allowed by applicable legislation, are some of the activities carried out during the screening.

Along with an owner and business license at the state and national levels, enterprises also need general liability insurance. The company receives a Guaranteed certified badge if it completes the entire process of screening.

Google Guarantee: Why Google Started It

Let's check out these scenarios to understand why Google started Google Guarantee.

Situation 1

Some businesses deceive their customers by submitting phony ratings and reviews to Google My Business alongside other citation websites. Google cannot confirm whether the reviews and ratings are from actual clients. Google created this tool to prevent this and give its users the finest home service possible.

Situation 2

You usually call a plumber to help with the water supply setup. This call could be frequently sent to offshore contact centers where leads are sold to an ambiguous plumber. After work is finished, you can receive a hefty fee for subpar work.

This situation applies to professions like contractors, landscapers, locksmiths, and handypersons. They promise no quality guarantees, only that individuals should spend as little as possible. Google created this initiative and awarded these neighborhood businesses for having certified Google Guaranteed identification badges to prevent this catastrophe.

What Sectors in the US are Eligible for Google's Guarantee?

A crucial thing to do if you need clarification on whether your company is eligible for the Google Guarantee program is to discover if you qualify. Google Guaranteed is available in the following sectors in the United States:

- Appliance Repair
- Financial planning
- Event planning
- Garage door installation
- Lawn care
- HVAC (ventilation, heating, and air conditioning)
- Pet grooming
- Water damage restoration
- Tree services
- Window repair and cleaning, and lots more

It understands the Process Involved in Getting Google Guarantee. Now that you know the fundamentals of Google Guaranteed, how does it operate?

Signing up for Google Service Ads is the first step to becoming Google Guaranteed (LSA). LSA will display essential company data, such as location, customer feedback, contact details, and operating hours. Background checks, proof of general liability insurance, and proof of business or owner licenses are all included in this. Your company will only be featured as Google Guaranteed if it has registered with LSA and undergone rigorous screening procedures.

Businesses must correctly maintain their status after receiving their Google Guarantee badge to keep it from being withdrawn. This includes keeping a valid license and insurance, updating your Google Business profile regularly, soliciting favorable reviews, answering critical comments, and checking for updates from Google.

How Can One Join Google's Guaranteed Program?

Google has developed a sophisticated verification system to give users a far better experience. You need to sign up for Local ads before you can be enlisted for this program. They make it simple for users to interact with your company. Your address, testimonials, location, and contact information will be displayed. Visitors can better comprehend your company's operations using this information.

- Start with legal local service advertisements.
- Obtain a clean background check.

- Check your insurance and license.
- Display of Google Guaranteed program individual listings

Google Guarantee Tips

This Google program can enable businesses to obtain qualified leads. As a result, maintain your business ready at all times by keeping in mind the following:

- Make sure your company has the necessary licenses and insurance.
- If not, asking the accountant to include the name utilized in the Google Listing effectively serves as an interesting name for the operation of the Business Incorporation document.
- Ensure that the Business Name in the Incorporation document corresponds with the name in the Google Listing.
- Have a certified Google My Business page that is constantly updated and verified.
- Request testimonials from happy clients, and don't ignore any complaints.

When your industry appears on our list, keep an eye out for updates to the Google Guaranteed register and reviews as quickly as possible.

The Google Guaranteed legal screening procedure could be challenging; however, it can significantly improve lead creation once the process is through. However, more than signing up for the program is required. It must be adequately maintained, or your Google identification badge can be removed. To increase your internet presence, abide by the guidelines set forth by Google.

Setting Up a Google Guarantee Application

It's simple to get the green checkmark next to your company name. Google offers a simple application form and clearly outlines the steps. Register for Google Local Services (formerly Google Home Services), submit a free background check, and verify your business license and insurance if you still need to.

Let's see how Google Guaranteed can be configured for your company. Thankfully, the procedure is simple; follow the three steps below!

Verify Your Eligibility

First, you should determine your eligibility before setting up Google Guaranteed. Ensure you're on the list first because not all business types have access to the badge yet. Currently, the following industries are eligible:

- Device Repair
- Vehicle glass
- Auto upkeep and repair
- Cleaning of rugs and upholstery
- Planning an electrical event Financial planning
- Installation of garage doors
- Domestic cleaning
- HVAC
- Removing trash
- Lawn maintenance
- Lock-picking services

- Pest Prevention

Don't worry if your industry still needs to be included in that list; Google constantly adds new sectors to Google Guaranteed. Just be aware of when yours becomes accessible!

Examine Your Credentials

When you apply for the Google Guaranteed badge, Google thoroughly investigates your company. It will verify your business license, insurance, and online reviews and explore the business owner (and occasionally extra employees). Review every piece of information you anticipate Google to look into to prepare for such checks.

Start by making sure your insurance and business license is current. Then check your internet reviews to see if they give your company a favorable impression. Before continuing the application process, focus on completing or improving any issues that aren't going well.

Submit Your Resume

You can finally submit your Google Guaranteed badge application after everything is in order! To ensure the badge is accessible in your location, you must first enter basic information about your company on the application. The remainder of the application is quick and easy once you finish the first section.

It can take some time before you hear back; Google needs to run its numerous background checks on your company so that it won't happen immediately. But eventually, if everything appears to be in order, it will let you know and hand you your badge! Once Google Guaranteed is set up, all that's required of you is to continue upholding the criteria that won you the badge in the first place.

The Google Guaranteed Badge: What Is It?

Wayne searches Google for a qualified local plumber to assist with fixing his plumbing because he needs it. And suddenly, he notices it. Your plumbing company appears in the results list, but with so many choices, Wayne needs help deciding which companies are trustworthy enough to contact.

There is a checkmark in a green circle next to your company, along with the words "Google Guaranteed," next to it. He recognizes that as a positive indicator before he understands it. After learning more, he is even more confident that choosing your company is the best move. The situation mentioned above may come to pass when you obtain the Google Guaranteed Badge for your company. It can do wonders for your web promotion and benefit people rushing to discover a reputable local business.

Google certifies specific neighborhood businesses with the Google Guaranteed emblem to reassure customers of the caliber of their offerings. This is Google's expression, "We promise this company will offer top-notch service." Users can use the badge to identify the most trustworthy establishments in their local searches.

Looking at which businesses in a list of several search results have the Google Guarantee can help you cut down your options. Of course, the badge serves purposes beyond those of prospective customers. It also helps the companies. When your business displays the Google Guaranteed badge, it's comparable to receiving the best recommendation.

Google immediately informs users that your company is reliable.

Where is the badge visible?

The Google Guaranteed badge mostly appears in two places:

Ads from local search

Rectangular boxes in the shape of local search ads are displayed above standard PPC ads. They include the emblem and essential details like the name of the company, its phone number, its hours of operation, and a star rating.

Business profile on Google

The badge for the relevant businesses can occasionally be shown next to their Google Business Profile, whether in Google Maps results or local search packs. Google Guarantee badge is the same in both places; it is a checkmark in a green circle with the words "Google Guaranteed" next to it.

How Much Does it Cost to Obtain Google Guarantee?

There are no click-through or view fees under Google's Guarantee program. Instead, companies pay for each sale lead they acquire via local service advertisements. You don't have to pay to obtain the badge to add it to your Local Services advertisements. Google Guaranteed may have a cost.

However, the setup fee for the badge is a flat rate of $50 per month ($600 per year) if you want to use it on your Google My Business profile. The service, location, location, and lead type of the business are only a few variables that affect the cost per lead. Direct messages, phone calls, voicemails, emails, text messages, and any other type of customer-business communication are all considered legitimate leads.

Owners can concentrate on their business because companies can set their budgets based on the monthly active leads they need. Before this, only companies who purchased Google Service Ads were eligible for the Google Guarantee. However, small firms that don't seem to be a part of the unique LSA program will now be actively offered a similar type of backing and badging for $50 per month.

Through organic search, firms can differentiate themselves from local rivals thanks to this monthly fee.

Google Guarantee Benefits for Businesses

A business with Google Guaranteed is guaranteed various benefits, including lead generation, enhanced search results rankings, and increased user confidence. Your company will be highlighted on the search engine's top result page as one of the Local Service Ads. This allows brands to connect with active users looking for your company's services.

Increased leads and conversions will follow from being a part of the top listings and having the verified and certified check mark. Additionally, when a user contacts you directly because of the advertisement, you only actively pay for measured outcomes.

Makes Service Ads Pop

Customers will notice a large green checkmark in addition to your service's average advertising rating. Thanks to this tick, your company can distinguish itself from rivals who aren't Google Guaranteed or Screened.

Google Image from April 2022 offers confirmation even through phone and audio searches. Customers hear proof that your company is Google Guaranteed in the United States only when they use voice search (like Google Home or Google Assistant) to discover the service they need.

With Keyword Hero, unlock (not provided)

View the exact performance numbers for your organic keywords in Google Analytics—no-cost trial. Anytime, cancel. Professional assistance. A four-minute setup Customers will remain covered by Google Guarantee when they call your company.

Manifests Your Concern for Your Company's Reputation

You must actively seek out fresh possibilities to increase your credibility. By completing the Google Guarantee certification procedure, you demonstrate to your clients that you are prepared to go above and beyond to guarantee their pleasure.

A further step in enhancing your customers' experience with the company from their search to purchase is completing the screening process.

Frequently Asked Questions on Google Guarantee

What is the price of Google Guarantee?

Like most Pay-Per-Click services, your costs may change depending on traffic requirements. Every business has a somewhat different starting budget, but we've seen as little as $25 to $50 each week! Your budget can be changed as necessary (more on that later).

What kind of licenses am I required to have for Google Guarantee?

Google confirms that advertisers maintain state, provincial, or national licenses for enterprises and owners/managers. Each advertiser's provider profile lists the licenses Google has established for that particular advertiser.

How do I set up insurance for the Google Guarantee?

Each provider's company must maintain general liability insurance coverage for all services rendered. When setting up your account, Google will need a copy of your insurance policy.

To my Google Guarantee listing, can I upload images?

You may use images in your listing. The size requirements for the photos on your Google Guaranteed profile are stringent. We can assist you in optimizing your profile for optimum impact.

Is Google Guarantee subject to a background investigation?

Yes, Google looks at the history of your business! You can get a background check conducted by "Evident" at no cost. Typically, this takes two to five weeks, depending on how quickly Google can reach everyone.

Can I alter my spending plan at any time?

Yes, that is part of its attractiveness. The budget can be adjusted and changed as necessary.

How can I tell if the Google Guarantee is effective?

Tracking is a cinch because Google will email you when a customer calls your company after seeing the Google Guarantee banner. Better more, Google records the calls so your business can actively train its callers and maximize its return on investment.

Can I pick the locations where I run Google Guarantee ads?

You may pick and choose which cities you want, yes. Thanks to this, you can precisely select the regions you want to focus on.

Can I pick the locations where I run Google Guarantee ads?

You may pick and choose which cities you want, yes. Looking at the map to the left, you may see how to select your destinations utilizing the Google Guarantee program. It's simple to use and makes it simple for you and your company to choose the zip codes you want to advertise in. Thanks to this, you can precisely select the regions you want to focus on.

What steps must I take to set up Google Guarantee?

Locate "Google Local Services" and sign in using your existing or new account as the first step. Following a series of inquiries, Google will determine whether or not you are eligible for the program.

Businesses have little choice but to adapt their marketing strategies to comply with Google's changes. Sign up as soon as you can to take advantage of Google Guarantee. If you don't have a storefront, it might be worthwhile to assess your resources and decide whether it would be a wise investment to have a business address different from your home address.

CHAPTER 13

Mistakes To Avoid

Google Business Profile can be one of the most valuable tools for any local business – one that can help you gain customers or clients and, most importantly, revenue.

You must start by auditing your listing and then addressing each problem accordingly. Here's a step-by-step guide for conducting a technical GBP audit.

Google Business: Technical SEO Audit Items

1. Brand Dilution Diagnosis

To ensure that Google assigns a certain amount of recognition or authority to your business, search for your business name on Google.

- Does the brand query serve as a Knowledge Graph?
- Do competitors or irrelevant results get served for the brand query?

If a Knowledge Graph is not showing up for your brand query and you only see irrelevant results, then the following solutions can help:

Brand Insulation: Leverage schema and data aggregation platforms to create and optimize authoritative profiles and social accounts.

Reverse-engineer your competitor's Knowledge Graph.

2. Address Audit

Some local business owners need to pay more attention to the accuracy of their business addresses in various online listings. Drop the address from your Google Business Profile listing to Melissa.com to determine if you have this problem. It will record any issues with the specific address your business is using.

You also want to look at your business pin in Google Maps and make sure it's inside of the actual city limits. Here are more tips to resolve and address issues:

- Fix non-existent suites.
- Update address formats.
- Modify expectations on service areas.

3. Fighting the 'Possum' Filter

Google may filter out low-quality or spammy-looking listings from local search results. Ensure your business doesn't have duplicate listings that might affect your visibility.

To check: Paste your business address into the Google Maps search bar.

Select the "Nearby" filter.

This presents every other business that's registered at that address. Duplicate listings are easy to handle when they're yours.

While it's not an easy problem to fix, you can mitigate practitioner listings with proper categorization. Creating a "filter flip" might help businesses located in large metro areas with competitors in the same building.

With this approach, your goal is to convince Google that your listing is more authoritative than the others at the same address.

4. Phone Number Health Check

Phone numbers can also cause problems with listings. To avoid them, you'll want to:

- Ensure multiple businesses aren't using the same number.
- Identify data consistency issues, business listing issues, etc.
- You can look up your phone number, using different variations, in Google to double-check your contact info's consistency.

Then using Google's advanced search operators, you can enter all as a search query.

5. Google Business Profile Listing Audit

Follow these tips to optimize your GBP profile:

- **Fill out your listing.** Feeding Google more data about your business helps you appear in relevant search results.

- Go the extra mile with attributes, images, Q&A, posts, reviews, etc. This helps you stand out in the local map pack.

- **Smart category optimization.** Find four of the most relevant categories to your business, and don't go beyond that. Stay as niche as possible to get quality leads from your listing.

- **For multi-location service-area businesses, follow the "radii rule."** If you're in one city and you have multiple locations, avoid overlapping with another one of your locations when creating your radius of the service area. These overlaps can cause visibility issues.

6. Local Signals

Focus on essential citations and niche directories like Yelp and Yellow Pages. Don't spend too much time on citations; start thinking about high-quality local signals. There are many ways to build hyper-relevant and geo-specific links that don't involve shady citation sites.

**Bonus Section on Google Ads PPC

Introduction to Google Ads PPC

Are you ready to expand your current digital marketing efforts?

Google's search engine receives an average of 40,000 searches per second. This means that it processes over 3.5 billion searches daily! Search engines like Google can be your key to a powerful and effective digital marketing strategy.

Paid advertising and Search Engine Optimization (SEO) can help maximize online audiences and increase your digital reach.

Google AdWords offers business owners an excellent means of paid online advertising. Google makes over $90 billion annually on ads alone!

Launching a Google AdWords campaign may seem intimidating if you're starting in digital marketing. However, you don't need a background in marketing to tackle AdWords. In this bonus section, I will show you all the basics of getting started.

You'll discover what Google Ads is and what you need to know to begin advertising on Google. This bonus section will educate you on creating successful Google Ad campaigns, using negative keywords, doing competitor research, setting up AdWords extensions, Ads bidding and pricing strategies, and more.

What are Google Ads?

Google Ads has become increasingly popular among businesses across all industries since they provide more robust and focused paid campaigns leading to a higher chance of getting more customers.

Google Ads is a paid advertising platform that falls under a marketing channel known as pay-per-click (PPC), where you (the advertiser) pay per click or per impression (CPM) on an ad.

It is an effective way to drive qualified traffic, or the right customers, to your business while they're searching for products and services like the ones you offer. With Google Ads, you can boost your website traffic, receive more phone calls, and increase your in-store visits.

Google Ads allows you to create and share well-timed ads (via both mobile and desktop) among your target audience. This means your business will show up on the search engine results page (SERP) when users aree looking for products and services like yours via Google Search or Google Maps.

Note: Ads from the platform can span across other channels, too, including YouTube, Blogger, and Google Display Network.

Additionally, no matter your business size or available resources, you can tailor your ads to suit your budget. The Google Ads tool lets you stay within your monthly cap and pause or stop your ad spending anytime.

Now, onto another essential question: Is Google Ads effective?

Do Google Ads work?

To answer this, let's consider a few statistics.

- Google Ads have a click-through rate of nearly 8 percent.
- Display ads yield 180 million impressions each month.
- For users ready to buy, paid ads on Google get 65% of the clicks.
- 43% of customers buy something they've seen on a YouTube Ad.

So, yes, Google Ads works. You can create a high-ROI marketing campaign with an optimized ad campaign and lead flow.

Why advertise on Google?

Google is the most used search engine, receiving 3.5 billion daily search queries. Not to mention, the Google Ads platform has been around for nearly two decades, giving it some seniority in the area of paid advertising. Google is a resource used by people worldwide to ask questions that are answered with a combination of paid advertisements and organic results.

And according to Google, advertisers make $8 for every $1 they spend on Google Ads. So, there are a few reasons why you'd want to consider advertising on Google.

Need another reason? Your competitors are using Google Ads (and might even be bidding on your branded terms). Thousands of companies use Google Ads to promote their businesses, which means that even if you're ranking organically for a search term, your results are being pushed down the page beneath your competitors.

Common Google Ads Terms you should Know

1. AdRank
2. Bidding
3. Campaign Type
4. Click-Through Rate
5. CPC
6. CPM
7. Conversion Rate
8. Display Network
9. Ad Extensions
10. Keywords
11. PPC
12. Quality Score

These common terms will help you set up, manage, and optimize your Google Ads. Some are specific to Google Ads, while others are generally related to PPC. You'll need to know these to run an effective ad campaign.

AdRank

Your AdRank determines your ad placement. The higher the value, the better you'll rank, the more people will see your ad, and the higher the probability that users will click your ad. Your AdRank is determined by your maximum bid multiplied by your Quality Score.

Bidding

Google Ads is based on a bidding system, where you, as the advertiser, select a maximum bid amount you're willing to pay for a click on your ad. The higher your bid, the better your placement. You have three options for bidding: CPC, CPM, or CPE.

1. **CPC, or cost-per-click**, is the amount you pay for each click on your ad.

2. **CPM, or cost per mille**, is the amount you pay for one thousand ad impressions; that is, when your ad is shown to a thousand people.

3. **CPE, or cost per engagement**, is the amount you pay when someone takes a predetermined action with your ad.

Campaign Type

Before you begin a paid campaign on Google Ads, you'll select between one of three campaign types: search, display, or video.

1. **Search ads** are text ads displayed among search results on a Google results page.

2. **Display ads** are typically image-based and are shown on web pages within the Google Display Network.

3. **Video ads** are between six and 15 seconds and appear on YouTube.

Click-Through Rate (CTR)

Your CTR is the number of clicks you get on your ad as a proportion of the number of views your ad gets. A higher CTR indicates a quality ad that matches search intent and targets relevant keywords.

Conversion Rate (CVR)

CVR measures form submissions as a proportion of total visits to your landing page. Simplistically speaking, a high CVR means that your landing page presents a seamless user experience that matches the promise of the ad.

Display Network

Google ads can be displayed on either search results pages or a web page within Google's Display Network (GDN). GDN is a network of websites that allow space on their webpages for Google Ads — these ads can be text-based or image ads and are displayed alongside content relevant to your target keywords. The most popular Display Ad options are Google Shopping and app campaigns.

Extensions

Ad Extensions allow you to supplement your ad with additional information at no additional cost. These extensions fall under one of five categories: Sitelink, Call, Location, Offer, or App.

Keywords

When a Google user types a query into the search field, Google returns a range of results that match the searcher's intent. Keywords are words or phrases that align with what a searcher wants to see information on. You select keywords based on which queries you want to display your ad alongside.

For example, a searcher that types "how to clean gum off shoes" will see results for advertisers that targeted keywords like "gum on shoes" and "clean shoes."

Negative Keywords are a list of keywords you want to avoid ranking for. Google will pull you from the bid on these keywords. Typically, these are semi-related to your intended search terms but fall outside what you offer or want to rank for.

For Example, a searcher types in "Paris"; of course, there is the city Paris and the person, Paris Hilton. If you are a tour guide company, you will want to use negative keywords relating to "Paris Hilton."

PPC

Pay-per-click, or PPC, is a type of advertising where the advertiser pays per click on an ad. PPC is not specific to Google Ads but is the most common type of paid campaign. It's essential to understand the ins and outs of PPC before launching your first Google Ads campaign.

Quality Score (QS)

Your Quality Score measures the quality of your ad by your click-through rate (CTR), the relevance of your keywords, the quality of your landing page, and your past performance on the SERP. QS is a determining factor in your AdRank.

How does Google Ads work?

Google Ads displays your ad to potential leads or customers interested in your product or service. Advertisers bid on search terms or keywords, and the winners are placed at the top of search results pages, on YouTube videos, or on relevant websites, depending on the type of ad campaign selected.

Start Your Campaign

Given its reach and authority, Google Ads should be a part of your paid strategy. There's no such thing as a Google Ads campaign that doesn't work — only ones that need more work. Using the strategy and information here, you can create an Ad campaign that drives clicks and converts leads.

Trend #1: Google Ads Smart Bidding

In recent years, Google has invested heavily in artificial intelligence (AI), and Smart Bidding is one of the many results of that investment.

Google's definition is:

'Smart Bidding is a subset of automated bid strategies that use machine learning to optimize for conversions or conversion value in each auction — a feature known as 'auction-time bidding.'

Google's AI system uses machine learning to optimize for conversions in each auction automatically. You tell Google your advertising goal, and Smart Bidding determines how to get it done within your budget.

Smart Bidding works for a few PPC goals, including:

- **Target CPA**: Generate new leads and customers for your desired cost per acquisition.
- **Target ROAS**: Get the best return on investment (ROI) on your spending.
- **Maximize Conversions**: Increase your conversion rate.

Smart Bidding allows you to use many different signals for your bid optimization, some unique to the system and unavailable with manual bidding.

Here are just a few of the signals you can choose from:

- **Location intent**: Where a user intends to go versus their physical location. For example, if someone is researching travel.
- **Weekday and time of day**: Local businesses can target customers during certain times with relevant information or offers.

- **Remarketing list**: Ads can be optimized based on when users last interacted with products and what those interactions were.
- **Ad characteristics**: If you have multiple versions of an ad, Google can bid on the ones most likely to convert.
- **Interface language**: Bids can be adjusted for the language a user searches for.

Machine learning enables Smart Bidding to manage several signals simultaneously and tailor bids to each user's context, so if a user is more likely to click on your ad while on the way home from work, Google can raise your bids for mobile ads between 5 and 6 p.m. on weekdays.

Smart Bidding is a great option for businesses just getting started with Google Ads or those who don't have much time to devote to managing a campaign. The main downside to using it is not having control over which third-party sites your ads display on — you have to choose all of them or none of them.

Trend #2: Google Discovery Ads

Google rolled out Discover, its personalized mobile newsfeed, in late 2018. The goal of the feed is to surface relevant content to users even when they're not searching:

Discover's content is arranged as cards under topics to explore and, depending on a user's interests, includes different types like videos, recipes, news articles, and blog posts. Because the focus of the content is relevancy, it doesn't always give you the newest content — typically, quality evergreen content is featured.

Google Discover is available via the Google mobile app and by visiting Google.com on a mobile browser. Users can control what shows up in the feed, which leads to a more personalized experience.

Earlier this year, Google introduced Discovery Ads, which are native ads that show up in multiple Google feed environments.

Similar to Display Ads or YouTube ads, Discovery Ads must be visually engaging and mobile-friendly to feel native to the feeds they are displayed on. Google uses machine learning to optimize ad placement based on user's search history, feed engagement, and other factors to deliver them to the most interested potential customers:

Google's Discovery Ads allow marketers to reach potential customers in the Discover feed, the YouTube home feed, and Gmail.

Trend #3: Expanded Audience Segments

Google is devoting a lot of time and resources to audience segments. Giving businesses more ways to target the right customer is a win-win proposition for Google because it benefits both the business and the user (not to mention Google's bottom line).

In October 2021, Google announced two expanded audience segments:

Affinity Audiences: These audiences are built around interests and identified based on browsing behavior. Some examples of Affinity Audiences are beauty mavens, convenience store shoppers, and cloud services power users. According to Google, Volkswagen used affinity audiences to achieve a 250% increase in conversion rates.

In-market Audiences: These audiences are actively researching or comparing products and services. Google recently rolled out new seasonal event segments for these audiences so that advertisers could reach consumers on search and YouTube with timely offers.

According to Google, Toyota saw a 67% increase in conversion rate and a 34% reduction in cost per conversion when they used the Black Friday and Christmas segments to focus on shoppers actively looking for a car. With more than 700 in-market audiences identified, many companies will have the chance to interact with customers ready to purchase.

Find these new audiences in the Ads UI:

Neither of these signals is brand new, but they have been expanded to allow businesses to hone in on their ideal customers at the right time. When setting up a new campaign, you can layer these audiences on top of your other parameters

Trend #4: Google Ads and Voice Search

As more and more people buy smart speakers and search Google on mobile, text-based search will continue to decline. And that will mean big trouble for advertisers. Consider these stats:

- 55% of all-American homes will own a smart speaker by 2022
- 72% of people who own voice-activated speakers say that their devices are used as part of their daily routines
- Voice shopping is set to jump to $40 billion in 2022, up from $2 billion today
- 2 out of 5 adults use voice search once daily

Currently, voice searches that use screens — such as Google voice search on a desktop or a phone — will display ads. But smart speakers like Google Home and Amazon Alexa devices don't. That's the bad news.

The good news? That will change. Google is already testing ads on Google Home. As users move away from text-based search, the tech giant will surely find ways to monetize voice search.

Create a Goal for Advertising

Before starting your AdWords campaign, it's essential to keep strategy in mind. Most marketing strategies begin with identifying the goal or the desired outcome.

Your goal at this stage in the game may be simple. You may be a start-up seeking any digital visibility.

However, do your best to choose concrete and achievable goals when developing a digital marketing strategy. This is particularly important when setting up an AdWords campaign.

The words you incorporate into one of these ads are more likely to resonate with viewers if an actionable goal backs them!

Create Interesting Online Content

When setting up a Google AdWords campaign, spending some time honing your digital content before launching any ads is critical. A successful ad does more than capture initial interest, after all. An effective digital ad should send users to a page that will continue to capture their interest and (hopefully) conversions.

Include Search Engine Optimization (SEO)

Note that "AdWords" is now "Google Ads."

This portion of your Google AdWords tutorial is essential. You may think, "We're already in position 3 and haven't even started our Google ads."

The more "pre-work" you can do for your AdWords campaign, the more likely you are to find success. This applies to any digital marketing campaign.

If you've already implemented SEO, check out the integrity of your keywords. If you are new to SEO, use Google's Keyword Planner to brainstorm trending keywords. This tool also integrates neatly with any AdWords campaign.

Make sure to optimize individual pages on your website for different keywords. This is more likely to result in a higher Google ranking, which can leverage your AdWords campaign further.

Gather a few local citations.

If you are a local business of any kind, gathering a few local citations is essential before launching an AdWords campaign. This means claiming a Google listing so you can appear on Google Maps and in local searches or creating a Google Business Profile as at the beginning of the book.

It also means setting up accounts on local review portals, such as Yelp, Angie's List, Yellow Pages, and TripAdvisor. Ensure that your contact information is consistent on all these platforms. Establishing a powerful local presence online can increase your digital visibility and leverage a paid advertising campaign.

Craft Individual Campaigns

Now that your online content is in prime condition for digital marketing, it's time to learn how to set up a Google AdWords campaign.

In general, we recommend starting with several different campaigns. For example, if you own an online clothing store, one of your campaigns may focus on advertising for "Women's Clothing."

Break these individual campaigns into ad groups themselves, which may include "Women's tops," "Women's professional attire," and "Women's pants." These Ad groups will then be broken down into different ads.

A consulting business, for example, may choose a campaign for "Digital Marketing Consulting." Ad groups for this campaign might include "SEO Consulting," "Content Strategy," and "Social Media Campaigns." When you set up your AdWords account, you can organize your campaigns this way.

Determine an overall Budget.

Most marketers designate a daily advertising budget and a bid amount. We recommend choosing a specific budget per campaign, particularly if you want to boost the visibility of a particular product over another. When making this decision, consider your advertising budget's long-term vision.

Whenever someone clicks on your Google ad, you must pay a "bid" price for that click. Thus, when setting up your AdWords campaigns, you must select a bid price for each campaign. This is the maximum amount you wish to pay per click.

Your overall budget will determine the bid amount you enter. But do keep in mind that bids can also determine your ad ranking.

Keywords Selection

Like your online content, Google ads are discoverable via popular keyword searches. As a result, any AdWords campaign requires a selection of keywords. Generally, the more competitive a keyword is, the higher its bid price is likely. In this case, your keyword and ads showing up will be affected by your daily budget.

Once you select your keywords, you have further options for boosting your ad's visibility. You can select different match types, for example, that help you further hone your target audience- a broad match keyword will enable your ad to appear for any searches that contain parts of the keyword in any order. Exact matches, on the other hand, are exactly what they sound like. Your ad will appear only when the exact keyword is searched.

Create a perfect Landing Page.

It is essential to decide where you want to send users once they click on your Google Ad. This is called your landing page. Many marketers will send users to the homepage of their websites, if applicable.

Others send them to more tailored content, such as a product information page or blog post. Considering your keywords and the ads' content is essential when deciding which landing pages to send users; choose the most relevant page. This is usually a page with more specific content than a homepage. In other words, you should create website landing pages for each ad group with specific keywords related to that ad group.

Write Your Ad Content

Keep your keywords and landing page information at hand as you craft your ad content. Don't forget about your campaign goals, either. Solid keywords can help make the writing of your ad content easier. Successful ads are concise, free of grammatical or spelling errors, and somewhat specific to the ad group.

The best ads will have some call for action in them. A call to action (CTA) can be as simple as a "learn more!" or "Shop sale items today."

Keep Tabs on Performance

Make sure that your Google AdWords account is linked to Google Analytics, a free tool that enables you to track your advertising performance through valuable metrics.

These metrics can help you further hone your campaign to generate results. They may help you modify your keyword selection or give you insight into the type of ad content you need to write. Metrics can also help you make the right financial decisions within the scope of your marketing budget.

Set Up A Google AdWords Campaign

Google should be a powerful component of every business's digital marketing scheme. If you've already taken advantage of SEO, it's time to harness the potential of Google AdWords.

Set yourself up for success by initially identifying your Google advertising goals. Ensure that your landing pages are optimized before launching any marketing campaign.

When you set up your AdWords account, craft individual distinct campaigns and make bid adjustments based on your budget and keyword popularity.

To succeed in any digital, radio, or PPC advertising, you must keep tabs on your competitors and their tactics. If they advertise on the subway, you should be too. Likewise, if they target a specific keyword in PPC, so should you.

There are a lot of free benchmarks for data available to all Google Ads users (formerly known as Google AdWords). Here are some great tools for analyzing your Google Ads competition.

1. Auction Insights

The Auction Insights report lets you look at who else is bidding on your keywords. You can see impression shares, average position, overlap rate, position above rate, and top-of-page rate each competitor has on a keyword. This information lets you better manage your bids and see your highest competition.

2. Keyword Planner

Typically, when people use the Google Ads Keyword Planner, they think of using it to find keyword ideas from their own site and landing pages. Conversely, try plugging a few of your competitor's URLs into the search bar. The results may display keyword ideas you never thought of using. Because these keyword ideas come from the competitor's site, they are likely already being utilized by your competitors.

You can also pay for many tools if your budget allows a little wiggle room, like SEmRush.

3.   Competitive Campaigns

Once your Google Ads account is well structured, you can think about optimizing it further with direct competitive advertising.

Another point is that Quality Score will be lower for competitive campaigns, and it is unlikely that your competitive campaign's ads will show up in the first position. After all, Google ensures that the searcher finds what they are looking for. However, it is essential to remember that there is no reliable data to prove that a higher position translates into a higher ROI.

As a side note, beware that when a business launches a competitive campaign on another brand, it is only a matter of time before the competitor is likely to launch their competitive campaigns in return.

On Google Ads, there are currently twelve different types of bidding that you can use for various goals.

1.   Target CPA (Cost Per Acquisition)

2.   Target ROAS (Return On Ad Spend)

3.   Maximize Conversions

4.   Enhanced Cost Per Click (ECPC)

5.   Maximize Clicks

6.   Manual CPC Bidding

7.   Target Search Page Location

8.   Target Outranking Share

9.   CPM Bidding (Cost Per Thousand Impressions)

10.   vCPM Bidding (Cost Per Viewable Thousand Impressions)

11.   CPV Bidding (Cost Per View)

12.   Target Impression Share Bidding

Google Ads Bidding, Option #1: Target Cost Per Acquisition (CPA)

Target CPA bidding is a bidding strategy you can use if you want to optimize conversions. If driving conversions are your primary goal for the campaign, selecting Target CPA bidding will focus on trying to convert users at a specific acquisition cost.

With this method, Google Ads will automatically set your bids on each campaign based on your CPA. While some conversions may cost more, others may cost less to even out and align with your acquisition costs.

Your Cost per Acquisition is simply the money you can spend to acquire one customer. For example, if you sell a product for $50, you don't want to set your target CPA at $50. That would be breaking even when the goal is to profit.

When selecting this bidding method, you can enter your target CPA and be ready!

Google Ads Bidding, Option #2: Target Return on Ad Spend (ROAS)

Target Return on Ad Spend is a bidding strategy that throws most for a loop. Because it requires some math. Yes, math the dreaded, awful subject that most marketers run from.

Unfortunately, math is essential on this one.

Target ROAS is the bidding strategy where Google Ads will set your bids to maximize conversion value based on the return you want from your ad spend. This number is percentage based.

Let me give you a basic example:

On your next Google Ads campaign, you want to generate $10 for every $2 spent. To do the math, you follow this formula:

Sales ÷ ad spend x 100% = Target ROAS

Doing the math for my example above, here is what the Target ROAS would look like:

$10 in sales from campaign ÷ $2 ad spend (clicks) x 100% = 500% target ROAS

Easy enough, right?

Here is what the Target ROAS bidding strategy looks like when creating a new campaign:

If you still aren't sure what to set as your percentage, you can navigate to a previous campaign on Google Ads and modify your columns.

Add the following metric to your columns:

Conv. value/cost

Use the number from your top-performing campaigns as your new Target ROAS.

Google Ads Bidding, Option #3: Maximize Conversions

Maximize Conversions is one of the simplest bidding strategies that Google Ads offers. Using the maximum daily budget you set, Google will automatically run your bidding to get you the most conversions for your money.

For example, if your daily budget is $50, Google will spend it wisely to find the most conversions. If a single conversion costs $50, Google won't bid on it for you.

Before selecting this bidding method, ensure that you set your daily budget amount at a reasonable level that you are willing to spend. At the end of a campaign, check your return on investment to see if maximizing conversions leads to profitable sales.

Google Ads Bidding, Option #4: Enhanced Cost Per Click (ECPC)

Enhanced CPC bidding is one of my favorite strategies on Google Ads. In a few words, using Smart Bidding, Google can increase or decrease your bid amount based on the likelihood of driving the sale. Bids will try to be about at your max cost-per-click settings.

If a search is too competitive and CPCs are outrageously high, Google can lower your bid to cost less due to decreased chances of converting. Google will make the call by increasing bids. This type of bidding is restricted to the Search and Display networks.

Google Ads Bidding, Option #5: Maximize Clicks

Maximize Clicks is an automatic bidding strategy based on your maximum daily budget. Google Ads will attempt to drive the most clicks possible with your daily budget.

Google Ads Bidding, Option #6: Manual CPC Bidding

Manual CPC Bidding gives you more control over your bidding strategy. But more control means more time spent monitoring costs and adjusting on your own. This strategy isn't your best bet if you aren't well-versed in Google Ads yet.

Manual CPC is where you set bids for different ad groups or placements. If specific campaigns are more profitable than others, you can quickly adjust budgets to add money or remove them from other campaigns.

You can also combine Manual CPC bidding with ECPC bidding:

Google Ads Bidding, Option #7: Target Search Page Location

TSPL (Target Search Page Location) bidding is the strategy of letting Google automatically adjust your bids constantly to show your ads either:

1.   On the first page results of Google

2.   At the top of the first page of Google (1-4)

While Google has the disclaimer that this strategy "doesn't guarantee placement," you won't have issues if your quality scores are solid.

Google Ads Bidding, Option #8: Target Outranking Share

Target Outranking Share is another automated bidding tactic perfect for competitor targeting on Google Ads. You can choose a specific website or competitor that you want to outrank.

When your ads and competitors' ads display, Google will increase your bids to outrank them. Google also will show your ads when your competitor isn't showing up to give you better brand awareness. Here are your options when selecting this bid strategy:

First, select the domain name you want to outrank. Focus on your biggest competitor, those you often notice on Google Ad results. Target to outrank is the percentage of times you want to bid to rank on top of them.

Google Ads Bidding Option #9: Cost Per Thousand Impressions (CPM)

Cost per Thousand Impressions, or CPM, bids solely based on impressions. This option is reserved for the Display Network and YouTube campaigns like TrueView and is not for use on the Search Network (for obvious reasons).

Google Ads Bidding Option #10: Cost Per Thousand Viewable Impressions (vCPM)

vCPM bidding is a tactic of manual bidding best reserved for brand awareness campaigns. Again, like CPM bidding, it is reserved for the Display Network. This bidding type sets your maximum costs on a viewable 1,000 impressions.

Google Ads Bidding Option #11: Cost-Per-View Bidding (CPV)

Cost-per-view bidding is strictly reserved for video advertising on Google Ads and can be used on the TrueView video platform. Using CPV bidding, you pay for video views or interactions. Interactions on the TrueView platform could be any of the following:

- Call-to-action clicks
- Overlay clicks
- Cards
- Companion banners

A "view" is determined by how long someone watches your video ad or the duration. In this case, with CPV bidding, a view is counted when someone watches 30 seconds of your ad or decides to engage!

CPV is currently the default setting for bid type on TrueView advertising. Let me give you a quick example of how it works. For CPV bidding, you enter the highest bid you will pay for a view or interaction. This is known as your maximum cost-per-view.

For instance, if you set your max CPV to $0.25, you would pay a maximum of 25 cents when a user watches your ad or engages with your call to action.

So, how do you know what to set as your CPV?

- Start low and adjust based on your results.
- Focus on first maxing out your quality scores and ad rank; these will drive down the cost-per-view on your ads, allowing you to pay less for better results.
- Slowly bump up your CPV to increase your audience reach.

Google Ads Bidding Option #12: Target Impression Share Bidding

Target Impression Share is a new bidding strategy released in late 2018 by Google Ads. This smart bidding strategy is focused on brand awareness and helping you reach as many people as possible.

As an example, if you are looking to dominate impressions for specific keyword searches, like basketball shoes, you can ensure your ads show up 100% of the time on SERPs by selecting 100% as your target impression share:

Target Impression Share is great if you want to build brand awareness but beware: The costs can add up fast if you select 100% on your targets.

This means you constantly bid to show your ads for a given term. Be sure to set a maximum limit and restrict your daily budget for this type of bidding. If you select to showcase your ads at the top of the page, you will pay more, too. Reserve this bidding type for cheap keywords and brand awareness goals.

Next step: Determine Your Google Ads Campaign Goals

Which bidding option is best for you? It all depends on your campaign goals. Every campaign you choose should carefully select a bidding strategy based on desired outcomes. Let's break down a few common goals on Google Ads and the top bidding tactics you can use for each.

Goal: Conversions.

If your goal on a specific Google Ads campaign is conversions or driving traffic to your website or store with the sole purpose of turning them into a sale, consider the following bid types:

- Maximize Conversions
- Target CPA
- Target ROAS
- Target Outranking Share (steal competitors' sales!)

Goal: Website traffic.

If you want to concentrate on driving more traffic to your site with goals other than merely converting, here are a few great bid types to choose from.

- Maximize Clicks
- Target Search Page Location
- Manual CPC Bidding

Goal: Brand awareness.

While brand awareness alone is a less common goal on the search network, there are a few great bidding tactics to utilize for maximum branding.

- Target Impression Share Bidding
- Target Search Page Location
- Target Outranking Share
- CPM and vCPM for YouTube and Display Networks

To make sure you're on the right path, follow these 4 Best Practices:

1. Always select a bidding tactic based on your campaign goals instead of flying blind and selecting the default option.
2. When push comes to shove, test different bidding strategies for a few weeks and see how performance changes.
3. Measure key performance indicators like conversions, conversion rate, cost per conversion, and more.
4. Stick with the one with better results!

Google Bidding Strategies: Conclusion

When launching a new campaign on Google Ads, choosing the perfect bidding format is complex. There are many options; if you don't have experience with each, the decision could make or break your campaign. Before selecting a bidding option, assess your goals.

If you don't structure your Ads account well enough or manage it effectively, the click-through rates of your adverts could be low. This means you won't get the traffic, inquiries, or sales you expected. So how do you improve AdWords CTR or click-through rates?

9 Ways to Boost Traffic and Improve Click-Through Rates.

1. Utilize all Ad extensions

Many ad extensions can make your advert stand out from the crowd. Using the full range of extensions increases the size of your ads and makes them appear more relevant, which, you've guessed it, improves the click-through rate.

There are many different types of Ad extensions, but the best ones are Sitelink ad extensions, Call extensions, Structured snippet extensions, Callout extensions, and Review extensions.

Many other extension types exist, including price, message, location, and app extensions. Depending on your advertising objectives, these will all help to increase the number of people clicking on your ads.

2. Write a persuasive Advert copy

It sounds simple, but unless you take the time to write engaging adverts that include strong calls to action, your advert performance will be average at best.

Look at your competitors' ads and try to write advert copy that stands out from the competition. Think about your business's unique selling points and experiment by split testing at least two adverts in every AdGroup

3. Include your target keywords in your adverts

If your adverts don't include the keywords you are bidding on within your advert copy, your CTRs will be poor, and you will potentially pay more than you need to. Include your target keyword in the headline, within the ad copy, and in the display URL.

4. Create tightly themed keyword groups

All the options in the Google AdWords interface are designed to encourage you to add multiple keywords to your account and your Ad Groups. The problem is that having 20+ keywords in an AdGroup impacts the relationship between advert text and keywords in each ad group.

When people search for a keyword in your Adgroup containing 20+ keywords, the advert that appears will, more likely than not, not contain the keyword they are searching for. The result is that your keywords and adverts' click-through rates and quality scores are adversely affected. The solution is to tight group themes or keywords into smaller groups and ensure that the advert copy contains the keywords at least twice if possible.

5. Use title case in your adverts!

Make your adverts stand out by using a title case. It is proven to increase AdWords CTR. Which advert stands out most from the selection below?

Example of two ads – one with title case in the headline and one without.

6. Use the advert display URL effectively

The display URL can reinforce the keywords used in your Ad Groups. Rather than display your actual website address, you can create an address that might not exist on your website but looks highly relevant to the search query you want your advert to display

You have 30 characters to use in the display URL in expanded text ads, which breaks down into two parts of 15 characters. Use the display URL to your advantage and include your ad group keyword phrases in parts 1 and 2 of the display URL.

Customize your AdWords display URL to boost CTR. You have 30 characters to include your keyword phrase on expanded text ads.

7. Regularly adjust your bids

Bid too low on your keywords, and your CTRs will suffer. Make sure that you regularly review your bid prices to ensure that you are bidding enough to appear on page one, and, secondly, your bids place you high enough on the page to get a decent click-through rate and, ultimately, cost-effective conversion rate.

Experiment with your bid positions and increase your bid prices incrementally rather than make bid increases. It isn't just about bidding to appear at the top of the page; this uses your budget and leads to expensive costs. Use Bid Adjustments when you know people are more likely to purchase.

8. Include calls to action and symbols in your advert copy

Think about your unique selling points and include them in your advert copy. This will make your adverts stand out and get more clicks. If you have something to shout about, such as an award or accreditation, include it in your advert copy or add site link extensions.

Using exclamation marks, @ symbols, and other characters can draw attention to your adverts and encourage clicks. Do be careful to stay within Google's advertising guidelines. You will generally only be able to use one symbol and exclamation mark per advert. Don't worry if you overdo it, as Google will indicate what you did wrong.

9. Check out the competition

If you are looking for ideas when writing new adverts, then why not start by looking at what your competitors are doing? How are they advertising? Do they focus on price or mention compelling, unique selling points? Are they using strong calls to action, site links, call extensions, or review extensions? Take inspiration from the best bits to create new adverts that stand out in the search results.

Which AdWords CTR improvement techniques work for you?

The above suggestions to improve AdWords CTR should undoubtedly help you to improve campaign performance. Experimenting and seeing what works for your site is a good idea. Once you've increased your traffic, you need to improve conversion rates.

What are Ad Extensions?

Ad extensions are additional features that you can add to your text ad. There is no additional cost to using extensions, but you must be in the top 3 spots to have them show. If you're not, then they won't display.

Some Ad extensions are just additional texts showing when someone sees your ad, while others are links people can click. When someone clicks on a site link or clicks to call, the cost is the same as if they'd clicked on the Ad.

Why Google AdWords Extensions Are So Important

The main benefit of Ad Extensions is that they make your ads stand out. According to Google, adding a new Ad extension to your ad can result in a 10-15% increase in click-through rate.

One advantage of extensions is that you can take up more real estate on the page, making your ad stand out. Google will show up to 4 extensions. This means your Ad could be nearly double the size of the ads below it. AdWords extensions allow you to provide more information about your business or the products or services you offer.

Ad extensions can potentially lower your costs by providing you with a better Quality Score. Google recently announced that these are a factor in determining Quality Scores. Having a higher Quality Score can often lower your cost per click.

How Google Ad Extensions Work and Which to Use

Here is a breakdown of the ad extensions currently available. The first three are extensions all businesses can use, while the rest will often depend on the type of industry you are in and your market.

1. Sitelinks

Sitelinks are additional links to your site. Instead of having prospects go to one page all the time, you can send them to various pages depending on their needs or interest. This is one of the best features to use as they also give more information about your business.

You can schedule some site links.

For example, a plumber can list emergency plumbing, sewer repair, grease trap cleaning, or other services. When looking for a plumber in an emergency, they may have more than a leaky faucet. It could be a backed-up sewer, and they'll click the ad of the plumber that lists that service and doesn't just say, 24-hour plumber.

When doing site links, you can include a more detailed description. They don't always appear in your ads, but they can make a difference when they do. So, think of them as each having their call to action and value proposition.

The title for each site link can be up to 25 characters, including spaces, while each description line can be up to 35 characters. Surprisingly you can use third-party sites as a site link to use one for your Facebook page and another for Twitter.

You can also send mobile visitors to a different page if you want. Click on Advanced options to find this option. Also under the Advanced option is the ability to add a start and end date for a specific link or to have it only run during certain hours of the day or certain days of the week.

You can do site links at the account, campaign, or ad group level.

Primarily for: all businesses.

2.   Callouts

You can add additional information with callouts. These can be used to highlight something about your company or a sale.

Callouts work for all businesses.

You have just 25 characters, including spaces, so it can seem restrictive. Ideally, you want at least 2 callouts, as they will rotate. One benefit, especially for sales, is that you can schedule them. You can also have separate callouts for mobile.

Callouts can add 10% to your click-through rate. As you can see, there is a significant increase in clicks using extensions.

As with site links, you can schedule a callout to run a short period, meaning they are ideal for specific promotions or limited-time offers. They can also be scheduled to run at certain times of the day. Finally, they can be used only for mobile, meaning you can call have a call to action specific to a mobile device, such as Call Us Today.

Primarily for: all businesses.

3.   Structured Snippets

Structured snippets are like a summary of the services or types of products you offer. There is a drop-down with a list of headings you can use, such as amenities, brands, courses, insurance coverage, and service catalog. After making your choice, you can create a list for your chosen category. You can start listing each brand on a line if you've chosen brands.

You must have three listings for each snippet, and you can have up to 25 characters for each listing. Google recommends having at least four listings.

Structured snippets are like a list.

Keep your snippets short despite the number of characters allowed so that more appear. Don't get clever with the titles but use straightforward descriptions.

Think of this as being like your website's navigation. If you have categories for your products or services, use these as the basis for your site link.

You can have more than one structured snippet in your campaign, although only one will ever show. So, if more than one of the categories applies to your business, use them. Then Google will choose which to display based on the prospect's search. Like callouts and site links, you have advanced mobile and schedule options.

Primarily for: all businesses.

4.   Call Extensions

In the past, you could put your telephone number in your ad, but this was prohibited with the introduction of call extensions. The trade-off, however, makes up for this. Now prospects can click to call your business instead of going through your website to make contact.

Often phone calls have a higher conversion rate than visitors who go to your site, especially if they're in a hurry to speak to someone such as a home service provider when they have a problem at home.

You can use your actual number or a forwarding number provided by Google. With this forwarding number, you can track the success of your ads.

You can also schedule call extensions, which is critical if you're phone is only answered at certain times of the day. Something else to remember about call extensions is that by using the call forwarding number, you can keep track of conversions that result from it being used.

Primarily for: service industries or businesses that sell products that a salesperson typically helps sell.

5.   App Extensions

With the app extension, you can either send interested prospects to your site for app information or allow them to download it directly by having them go to google play. For this extension to work, you must have your app available to download in either Google Play or the Apple App Store.

You can have several apps in your account, but only one will show at a time. When setting up the link, you choose your mobile app platform, either IOS or Android.

Then you look for your app by entering its name, package name, or publisher. Then you decide what the text link will be. The default is download now, but you can make it anything, with up to 25 characters available.

Primarily for: any business that has an app.

6.   Location Extensions

Google locations work with Google Business Profile

Location extensions are great for businesses with a physical location or wanting to show they're in the community they're targeting.

To utilize location extensions, you must have a verified Google My Business listing for each location you want to use and must have it verified in the same account as your AdWords account. Or at least know the email address of the account the listing is verified in.

Primarily for: businesses that have a brick-and-mortar location.

This extension applies to major retailers and auto dealers. After choosing one or the other, you'll see a list of the brands available under that category and by country. You add this location extension at the account level.

Primarily for: businesses that sell products in a store.

7. Promotion Extension

With promotion extensions, you can highlight a sale that is going on or special promotion going on with your business. One nice feature is that they are set to run specific days, highlight the promotion dates and the discount or savings amount, and take them to a specific page on your site with further information.

You can have a variation on the promotion specific to mobile. You can even have a special designation if it's for a holiday such as Valentine's Day or Black Friday. This extension won't be available if you use the old AdWords interface. It's only in the new interface.

You have four promotion types: Monetary discount, Percent discount, Up to monetary discount, and Up to percent discount. With this extension, you have up to 20 characters to describe the promotion and a link to a page on your site about the campaign.

You can also provide a promo code or a set amount (on orders) that people must spend to get the promotion. As with many other extensions, an advanced tab allows for special promotions on mobile, a start and end date, and scheduling.

Primarily for: products and services that utilize discounts or sale prices.

8. Message Extensions

This is the least used of the extensions. As one would expect, this only shows up on mobile.

It allows prospects to text a business directly with a question or a request. You must input your business name, the number to receive the text, and an extension text message like Text Us. A message text also only appears when a person clicks on the extension.

This is an excellent way for prospects who want to connect with you but don't necessarily want to talk to you over the phone. You also don't have to respond immediately to a message but can place it in a queue.

You are given another 100 characters to help users begin a conversation, such as hours. Message extension can be used across a campaign or ad group. This is another extension you can schedule. Its cost is the same as any click. Google keeps track of your messaging for your records.

Although many national businesses might find it helpful, it is primarily for local businesses.

9.   Price Extensions

This one probably takes the most work of all the extensions, but selling products or services at a fixed price is worth it. Think of them as site links for your products or services.

You can use them to list some of your products and include their price and a link to a page on your site where the product or service is available. You can list your services and the cost for local businesses such as hair salons.

You have 25 characters for the header of what you sell. Be careful, however, as they often shorten this, as you can see from the example below. Then you have the price and add a value, such as hourly or monthly.

You can add up to 8 products or services, and prospects can scroll through them. At a minimum, you must use at least four. You can add them at the account, campaign, or ad group level.

You can also send prospects to one page if they're on mobile and a different URL if they're on desktop.

Primarily for: businesses that sell products or have services with a fixed rate.

10.   Dynamic Extensions

In addition to the many extensions you can create, there are additional ones that Google can create independently. These are usually for businesses that don't currently use extensions. If you create your extensions, those will be shown above dynamic extensions.

Since you have no control over these, we'll only briefly mention the ones currently available.

- Call Extensions - These are used if you're not already using call extensions.
- Message Extension – Allow for the texting of messages provided you are using a mobile number for your call extensions.
- Dynamic Site Links - Google may decide that other pages might be more relevant to show underneath the ad.
- Structured Snippets – Again, Google will create a category and listing for your ads.
- Automated Location Extensions - another one that appears more often if you're not utilizing it.
- Seller Ratings - These are reviews that people have left about your business on Google. With the ending of the extension of the review, this one should be close behind.
- Callout Extensions – Again, Google creates something based on your current campaign and site.

Make Sure You Update Your Extensions Regularly. The best option is to incorporate the information in your extensions that aren't already in the ad's text. You should be if you still need to utilize Ad Extensions. They can take some time to set up, particularly if you have a number you can use. Yet, once done, they can not only make your ad look more robust, but they can allow you to let prospects know what makes your business unique.

Determining your most profitable keywords and creating relevant ad groups, ads, and landing pages based on those keywords is crucial to succeeding in paid search. Doing so lets you find potential customers searching for services or products like yours. But unless you've got money to burn, it's equally important to identify and eliminate keywords—and thus, searchers—who aren't looking for the products or services you provide.

Sadly, most Google Ads (formerly known as Google AdWords) and Bing campaigns cost far more than they need to because advertisers end up paying for clicks that never deliver a return on their often-substantial investment. For some, this can be frustrating enough to stop advertising on search networks entirely.

So how do you avoid the pitfall of wasted spend?

You use negative keywords, of course!

After reading what follows, you'll understand:

- Exactly what negative keywords are
- How can they improve the value and relevance of your paid search marketing efforts
- The value of negative keyword lists
- How to find and add negative keywords at scale

What Are Negative Keywords?

Negative keywords prevent your ad from showing to people who search for or browse content related to those words. Negative keywords allow you to do just that, ensuring your ads reach only the best potential audience.

Like the keywords you bid on, negative keywords can be assigned at the account, campaign, or ad group level and come in multiple flavors: broad, phrase, and exact. Understanding how these match types work is imperative to maximize the value of negative keywords in your Google Ads and Bing ad accounts.

Negative keyword match types

When using a broad negative match, your keywords are matched to multiple variations of a phrase, not all of which will be logical extensions of the phrase you're targeting or pertinent to your business.

In the example below, the negative broad match keyword running shoes would negate queries that show the entire negative keyword, even in cases where the words aren't in the same order.

This does not mean you will eliminate all relevant search queries; your ads will still be eligible to enter an auction if they contain some (but not all) of the terms in your negative keyword. This is illustrated in the example above, where an ad would still be served for search queries like "blue tennis shoes" and "Google running gear."

Negative phrase match keywords are slightly less restrictive.

Using the same example as before, your ads would be eligible to show for any search query that doesn't contain the phrase "running shoes." That's because this iteration only negates search queries that contain the exact phrase you specify. A search query could have more words than your negative phrase match keyword, but your budget is safe if it contains the exact phrase you've specified.

Finally, negative exact match keywords exist solely for you to eliminate specific search queries. If you add negative exact match keywords to your Google Ads account, your ads won't show only when a searcher enters exactly what you've added to your account. No extra words. Nothing.

Regardless of which network you're advertising on, you should be aware that adding too many negative keywords can hurt your ability to reach prospects; a carefully curated list, however, can save you a ton of money.

More advantages to adding negative keywords

Improve Click-Through Rate (CTR) — Ensuring that your ads aren't running against irrelevant queries means exposing your account to fewer uninterested impressions, meaning that the percentage of people who click on your ad will be more significant.

Create More Relevant Ad Groups — By weeding out keywords that aren't related to your business, you tighten the relevance of your ad groups. Small, closely related ad groups allow you to craft a single message that speaks to the entire group of keywords.

Save Money (Again) — So nice that it's listed twice! By avoiding paying for useless clicks, you save money by weeding out searchers who aren't a fit for your business. You can also avoid bidding against yourself, cannibalizing impressions, and watering down your keyword-level data.

Raise Your Conversion Rate — Negative keywords will ensure that your ads don't show for particular terms you know won't convert, like the names of competitors or those that convey a total lack of commercial intent.

How to Add Negative Keywords

So, you want to implement broad and phrase-match keywords in your account to capture more traffic, but you're left with a burning question...

How do I combat irrelevant clicks and impressions and uncontrolled ad spending?

Discovering negative keywords has been laborious, involving sitting around and brainstorming (which only gets you so far) or poring through search query reports in Google Ads.

To do this, navigate to the "Keywords" tab in the Google Ads UI at the account, campaign, or ad group level.

The default interface here will allow you to look at the keywords you're bidding on but not the queries that triggered them. To see this information, click "Search Terms" at the top of the UI:

Here, you'll notice columns that don't exist on the keyword screen, including:

- Search Term: The query a searcher entered into Google (or said to a virtual assistant) that triggered a keyword you're bidding on.

- Match Type: The degree to which a search query matches up with one of your keywords.

- Added/Excluded: Action you've taken with a search query (added it to your account or added it as a negative keyword)

Creating Lists of Negative Keywords

Let's face it: a Google Ads account built solely on exact match keywords probably isn't even effective if you're Ford or BMW. As such, you must rely on broad and phrase-match keywords to ensure adequate search volume and uncover new opportunities. But there is, of course, a downside to this sort of fishing expedition: you're probably competing for the same impressions across campaigns.

Let's say you sell cat and dog clothes through your eCommerce website.

Without negating the word cat (and all cat-adjacent queries) in your dog clothes campaigns, you'll inevitably run into the issue of Google deciding to match a broad match cat keyword to a dog-related search query. The results will be irrelevant to the searcher. If they don't click it, your CTR is watered down over time; if they do, the resulting landing page will have nothing to do with the search intent.

This is called a lose-lose.

Effective negative keyword management keeps your keyword research clean and maximally relevant, so you can deliver a compelling, targeted message to the exact segment of searchers you most want to reach. And your budget will be spent on impressions and clicks to drive relevant traffic, qualified leads, and eventual sales.

How do you avoid common mistakes and use AdWords as one of your company's most powerful marketing tools?

Look at the list of the five most common Google AdWords mistakes, never repeat those and observe the ever-increasing KPIs of your campaigns.

1. Not having a campaign strategy

A strategy is key in all marketing projects, including Google AdWords campaigns. At the very beginning, when you start to create an AdWords campaign, answer a few questions which are crucial for efficient campaign planning. At this stage, specify, among others:

- Campaign objectives.
- Target group.
- Expected results.
- Budget;
- Campaign duration.

Knowing the answers, you can choose the most appropriate type of AdWords campaign, determine the most effective way to target your ads, and design and select relevant landing pages. You can measure your campaign effectiveness, indicating how good — or bad — the results are.

2. Targeting AdWords campaigns to everyone

When creating a campaign to acquire new clients, you must remember that at least a few different audience segments can be targeted. Those are people looking for different information, using other keywords to find the information in the search engine, or visiting diverse websites to find restaurants in the area.

Thanks to the detailed segmentation of your target group and the creation of various campaigns of recipients (distinguished by similar features), the appropriate structure of your campaign can be designed.

3. Not having a dedicated landing page

If you run an AdWords campaign for the first time, you don't want to allocate a massive budget and resources — including time and your business staff — without knowing what the results will be. So, you start a campaign that leads your customers to your company's homepage.

The need for dedicated or appropriately optimized landing pages is one of the main reasons for low-performing ads.

WEBSITE AUDIT

Whether the purpose of a given AdWords campaign is to obtain registration for an industry conference or to sell products online, before you increase the website traffic, you need to be sure that this particular landing page is well-optimized to achieve your business goal. Conduct a website audit to analyze the technical and content aspects of the site and learn how to use optimization techniques to improve conversion.

Often minor changes in website content and functionalities of the landing page result in a significant improvement in campaign performance and ROI.

4. Skipping A/B tests and avoiding optimization

To achieve the best possible results of your AdWords efforts, you must systematically monitor your campaign performance, collect data, make conclusions, and implement changes.

At the beginning of the campaign, set out the hypothesis you want to validate and carry out A/B tests. A/B tests are one of the most effective optimization tools for every advertising campaign. When carrying out A/B tests, you can easily verify which of the two elements affects the target group better so that you achieve the best possible results. Simple enough!

Monitor the most effective content and which landing page gets the best traffic. Collect data, analyze all the insights, and use your knowledge to improve your advertising activities regularly.

5. Focusing on a conversion without analyzing additional KPIs

For various industries or types of campaigns, a conversion can include events such as a visitor filling out a contact form, newsletter form, registration form, or product purchase form in the online store. For different products or services, the conversion path may vary in length, including the time of making a purchase decision.

If the conversion is a visit to a site, it's relatively easy to measure the results of a given campaign. However, if your goal is to sell consumer electronics goods — e.g., new smartphone models — it's crucial to remember that purchasing decisions are rarely made when the user sees the ad or visits the online store for the first time.

The key is understanding the purchase path for a given product or service, its stages, and specificity, and on this basis, designing a multi-channel sales funnel.

Therefore, in addition to the conversion results — and ads quality — evaluate the traffic quality on the landing page. Understanding users' behavior and the purchasing process will allow for measuring the campaign results correctly and designing the sales funnel's further stages.

You should know This essential information when creating or optimizing an AdWords account. I have an entire book dedicated to Google Adwords PPC, GEOFENCING, Display Ads, Video Marketing, and Remarketing.

Check out the information on my Live Workshops on Google PPC, Deisng Your Own Website, and Digital Marketing.

You can find the current updated list of workshops at www.digitalwisemedia.com/events

About the Author Jennifer Martin

Jennifer Martin is an Author, Speaker, Business Coach, and serial entrepreneur, founder of several startups, including JustBoujeeLearning.com, DigitalWise Media, and MetaVerse Marketing Society, and hosts the "Boujee Lifestyle" Podcast.

She is a certified Google instructor and a digital marketing strategist—featured in the Dallas Morning Star on CNN, FOX, and the New York Times. She has also been seen worldwide, including on Today Tonight Show in Australia, TBS in Toyoko, and several others.

Listen or watch Jennifer Martin weekly on Boujee Lifestyle, the podcast where she talks about everything from her books, current events, business and marketing, leadership, and physical & mental health—being a mom, Boss Girl, and traveling. There is not much she doesn't cover in one of her episodes. Guests appear; most podcasts are recorded and streamed live on Instagram, YouTube, or Facebook.

When she is not writing, coaching, or creating a podcast, you can find Jennifer at the beach, drinking coffee, traveling, and with her laptop in hand, wherever that may be.

To be notified of new podcasts, live events, and author signing events, subscribe to Jennifer's updates at

https://jennifermartincoaching.com/about-jennifer

https://boujeelifestyle.com

Follow Jennifer on Facebook, Twitter, and Instagram for daily updates, plus Tiktok.

@realjennmartin and @BoujeeLifestyle

Her current speaking schedule, workshops, podcast schedule, and book release dates are on her company website at: https://digitalwisemedia.com.

Enjoy this book and pick up a copy of the other books written by Jennifer Martin.

About Boujee Publishing

Boujee Publishing is located in Houston, Texas.

Main 512-379-8888

Fax 512-379-8880

Info@boujeepublishing.com

To schedule a book signing with an author, contact our office. To see current events and signings scheduled, please visit our website. For information on publishing your book with Boujee Publishing, contact our sales department or visit our website:

https://boujeepublishing.com/publish

Boujee Publishing offers complete services for book publishing:

All Authors Receive the following Services:

- Book Editing and Formatting Services to your desired printed size.
- eBook formatting and distribution
- Cover Design, Bio & Descriptions
- Complete Author Website, Optimized for SEO and Google
- Google Knowledge Panel for Authors

- Amazon Author Page
- Goodreads Author Page
- ISBN and barcode for each format of your book
- Press Releases, Author Copies, Author Media Kits
- Scheduled Book Signings at Various Locations and Book Stores.
- Distribution to bookstores in the USA and Canada worldwide is also available.
- Professional author photos, Book Copies, Website photos, marketing images, BIO images, and branding packages.
- Complete Branding and Identity Packages
- Printed Collateral, Flyers, postcards, event planning, and schedules.

Also included is our Social Media bundle with Author Pages & Facebook & Instagram, plus 90 days of pre-book promotions and presales countdown on the website and social media.

Also, enjoy six months of social media posting for you, including high-quality graphics, images, and book promotions.

For more information on our Author package, please get in touch with us and see more details on our website.

http://boujeepublishing.com/publish

Made in the USA
Columbia, SC
08 November 2023

25740404R00111